Physics and Politics

PHYSICS
and
POLITICS

---

*Or: Thoughts on the Application of the
Principles of "Natural Selection" and
"Inheritance" to Political Society*

Walter Bagehot

WITH AN INTRODUCTION AND NOTES BY
Roger Kimball

Ivan R. Dee
CHICAGO

Library of Congress Cataloging-in-Publication Data:
Bagehot, Walter, 1826–1877.
  Physics and politics / Walter Bagehot : with introduction and notes
by Roger Kimball.
    p.   cm.
  Includes index.
  ISBN 1-56663-221-8 (alk. paper)
  1. Political science. 2. Nationalism. 3. Evolution.
I. Kimball, Roger, 1953– . II. Title.
JC223.B14 1999
320'.01'1—dc21

                                                    99-19271

Contents

Introduction

by ROGER KIMBALL

There are few ways in which a man can be more innocently employed than in getting money.
—Samuel Johnson, *Boswell's Life of Johnson*

The essence of civilization, as we know, is dullness. In an ultimate analysis, it is only an elaborate invention . . . for abolishing the fierce passions, the unchastened enjoyments, the awakening dangers, the desperate conflicts, . . . the excitements of a barbarous age, and to substitute for them indoor pleasures, placid feelings, and rational amusements. That a grown man should be found to write reviews is in itself a striking fact. Suppose you asked Achilles to do such a thing, do you imagine he would consent?
—Walter Bagehot, on Matthew Arnold (1853)

Only a blockhead can fail to realize that our characters are the result of our conduct.
—Aristotle, *Nicomachean Ethics*

I N THE large catalogue of half-forgotten Victorian masterpieces, Walter Bagehot's *Physics and Politics* (1872) occupies a distinguished place. Like its author, this short book is difficult to categorize. Informed by the burgeoning science of ethnology and the reinvigorated science of natural history, it belongs to neither. It might be described as a work of political psychology, but it is better written, rhetorically more astringent, and possessed of greater common sense than most works belonging under that rubric. Bagehot himself—part professional banker, part magazine editor, part cultural and political commentator —was also more than the sum of his parts. He once enjoyed a justly deserved reputation as a canny student of human nature. For many readers today, however, he is little more than an historical worthy: a name attached to a handful of epigrams. The historian Jacques Barzun, who introduced an edition of *Physics and Politics* in 1948, got it exactly right when he noted that Bagehot is "'well-known' without being known well."

In fact, Bagehot is one of those distinguished literary figures who seems to have been embalmed by his own distinction. There are no doubt many reasons for this. In his essay "Bagehot as Historian" (1968), Professor Barzun mentions two: he bore a name that was "puzzling to pronounce"—this made people shy about quoting him— and he made the mistake of dying at the inconsiderate age of fifty-one, before his idiosyncratic genius could take firm root in the popular imagination. Bagehot—the first syllable is pronounced like "badge," the second like "it": "badge-it"—has consequently had the misfortune to become more celebrated than he is read and discussed.*

---

* One occasionally hears "Bagehot" pronounced with a hard "g." But as the scholar Norman St. John-Stevas observes in *Walter Bagehot: A Study of His Life and Thought Together with a Selection from His Political Writings* (1959), "this is mistaken. It should be pronounced soft as in *badger*, which was indeed a fifteenth-century variant of the family name."

The misfortune affects the reading public as much as it does Bagehot's posthumous reputation. To miss out on Bagehot is to miss out on one of the great triumphs of English prose. It is a light, champagne prose: sparkling but not facile, broadly allusive but never pedantic, witty and epigrammatic but shrewd, strong, and sober enough to treat an extraordinarily wide range of serious issues. And treat them it does. Bagehot's prose is more than an aesthetic delight: it is a repository of uncommon wisdom about the common realities of life. The excellence of his writing, in other words, is an excellence of substance as well as style, matter as well as manner. What he says, he invariably says well; but one generally also finds that it is well that he said what he did.

During his brief lifetime, Bagehot's essays exerted an enormous influence. He had keen and original things to say about literary figures from Shakespeare and Milton to Shelley and Henry Crabb Robinson, the eccentric friend of Goethe, Schiller, Wordsworth, and Coleridge. Bagehot wrote penetrating essays on Adam Smith, Macaulay, Gibbon, Disraeli, Sir Robert Peel, and the English reformer John Bright. His speciality, as one critic observed, "was the human element in all the affairs and institutions of life, whether it relates to literature, history, politics, economics, sociology, religion, or science."

Talent has a way of commanding opportunity. At the end of 1851, the young Bagehot went to Paris to escape a bout of melancholy and indecision about his future career. Louis Napoleon just then embarked on the *coup*

Citing local and family testimony, St. John-Stevas is right that evidence for the soft "g" is "overwhelming."

d'état that marked his elevation from president of the Second Republic to Emperor Napoleon III. Bagehot's eyewitness dispatches to a London newspaper on the *coup* and its aftermath turned out to be a classic of pugnacious political reporting.

In 1867, Bagehot published *The English Constitution* (serialized the preceding two years in Anthony Trollope's *Fortnightly Review*), a work that is still regarded as an indispensable account of the workings of the English government between the first and second Reform Bills (1832 and 1867). Like many of Bagehot's works, *The English Constitution* is about much more than its announced subject. This gives it a relevance far beyond its time. Indeed, parts of the book might be even more pertinent now, 130 years later, than they were when first published. One cannot help thinking that Prime Minister Tony Blair and what remain of the Windsors could profit greatly by meditating on Bagehot's reflections on the importance of preserving the charm and mystery—what Bagehot referred to as the *impressive* as distinct from the *effective* aspects—of the monarchy. "We must not let in daylight upon magic," he wrote in a famous passage. "We must not bring the Queen into the combat of politics, or she will cease to be reverenced by all combatants; she will become one combatant among many." *Autre temps, autre moeurs*—or should one say, *plus ça change. . . ?*

Bagehot seems incapable of writing a dull sentence—a somewhat paradoxical situation, perhaps, since dullness was a virtue that he much applauded. Whether the subject was the American Civil War—about which he wrote nearly forty articles—parliamentary reform, or the workings of the London money market, he was sure to be bold, memorable, and pertinent. He was particularly pertinent when reflecting on the psychology of politics: the lineaments of leadership and motivation. Bagehot pondered deeply on the human requirements of civilization. He understood that personality often counted more than policy. "It is the life of teachers which is *catching*, not their tenets," Bagehot noted in *Physics and Politics*. The influence of personal example is one reason that what we have come to call the "character issue" has always been so important in government: "In political matters, how quickly a leading statesman can change the tone of the community! We are most of us earnest with Mr. Gladstone; we were most of us *not* so earnest in the time of Lord Palmerston. The change is what everyone feels, though no one can define it." A quick look at Washington, D.C. in the late 1990s shows that Bagehot's observation remains as true today as it was when he wrote it.

Bagehot did not simply comment on events from afar. As editor of *The Economist*—a position he held from 1861 until his untimely death—his advocacy of free trade helped to shape the financial policies of England at the zenith of her power. Gladstone was one of many politicians from both parties who sought his counsel. He became, it has been frequently observed, a kind of "supplementary Chancellor of the Exchequer." In an essay published in 1948, the eminent Victorianist G. M. Young, after duly reviewing the obvious candidates for the title of "The Greatest Victorian," finally awarded the palm to Bagehot. "One needs a man, or woman," Young wrote, "who is typical of a large and important class: rich in the abilities which the age fostered: one who made a difference, and under whose influence or direction we are still living." George Eliot, Tennyson, Arnold, Ruskin, or

Darwin may each have made greater contributions in his own line; the title *Victorianorum maximus*—greatest of the Victorians—may belong to one of them. But Bagehot's all-round genius, Young concluded, entitles him to the title *Victorianum maxime*, "The Most Victorian."

Many distinguished personages have agreed. Woodrow Wilson, for one, was smitten with Bagehot, calling him "a seer" and "one of the most original and audacious wits that the English race has produced." Of course, it would be unfair to hold Bagehot accountable for all of his enthusiasts. But it is remarkable how intense his appeal has sometimes been. The first collection of his works was issued not by a university or a commercial press but by an American corporation. In 1889, at the direction of its president, the Travelers Insurance Company published *The Works of Walter Bagehot* in five volumes and sent copies to its policyholders—the idea being, perhaps, that imbibing Bagehot's common-sense reflections on the human condition would make people better insurance risks. Doubtless it does.

Bagehot possessed abundantly a gift he discerned in Shakespeare: an "experiencing nature." He delighted in what he called "the grand *shine* on the surface of life." A central word for him is "enjoyment." Keenly moral, he abominated moralism: "Nothing is more unpleasant," he wrote, "than a virtuous person with a mean mind." Likewise, though formidably learned himself, he regularly cautioned against bookishness. "He wrote poetry . . . before breakfast," Bagehot wrote of Robert Southey with undisguised contempt; "he read during breakfast. He wrote history until dinner; he corrected proof sheets between dinner and tea; he wrote an essay for the 'Quarterly' afterwards; and after supper by way of relaxation

composed the 'Doctor.'" Bagehot's sense of ironical contrast was indefatigable. Comparing Gibbon's ornate style
with the world-shaking events he described in *The
Decline and Fall of the Roman Empire*, Bagehot observed
that perhaps "when a Visigoth broke a head, he thought
that was all. Not so; he was making history: Gibbon has
written it down." In a biography published in 1915, Mrs.
Russell Barrington, Bagehot's sister-in-law, frequently re-
marks on his boyish sense of fun. At breakfast once with
a young nephew struggling to open an egg, Bagehot ad-
vised: "Go on, Guy, hit it hard on the head. It has no
friends."

In politics Bagehot was a conservative Liberal. He sup-
ported a robust military but was broadly anti-imperialist.
Unlike many conservatives today, in Bagehot's time Tories
tended to favor economic protectionism and oppose free
trade. A student of David Ricardo's and Adam Smith's
writings on economics, Bagehot understood the important role that free trade played in fostering general
economic prosperity. Consequently he was an enthusiastic
supporter of policies that encouraged free trade. But even
here he was the opposite of doctrinaire. He understood
that a policy of "free trade" was one thing in the economic sphere, quite another when generalized to the
whole of life. Writing in 1848, he noted that the principle
of *laissez-faire* is "useful and healthy when confined to its
legitimate function, *viz* when watching that Government
does not assume to know what will bring a trader in
money, better than he knows it himself; but it is a sentiment very susceptible of hurtful exaggeration: in the
minds of many at this day it stands opposed to the enforcement of a moral law throughout the *whole* sphere of
human acts susceptible of attestation."

In the end, Bagehot is probably best described as a Whig with Tory leanings. How significant were those leanings may be gleaned from his observation (in the context of a discussion of the "Cavalier mind" and Sir Walter Scott, one of his favorite authors) that "the essence of Toryism is enjoyment." Bagehot gloried in the pulse, the vitality of life; he had little time for people or policies "sicklied o'er with the pale cast of thought," or with anything else, for that matter. The other side of this heartiness was an impatience that could sometimes border on callousness. "Ugly men," he wrote in his essay on Milton, "are and ought to be ashamed of their existence." Bagehot was loath to entertain, let alone dwell on, life's failures. Poverty, he remarked in a prickly essay on Dickens, is "an unfit topic for continuous art."

It is in this sense that Bagehot represents what one critic called "a standing temptation to indulge in selective Victorianism," accentuating the positive and—though not ignoring the negative—tending to dismiss it as a regrettable necessity. "The best history," Bagehot wrote in *Physics and Politics*, "is but like the art of Rembrandt; it casts a vivid light on certain selected causes, on those which were best and greatest; it leaves all the rest in shadow and unseen." And again: "The difficulty in truth is in the existence of the world. It is the fact, that by the constitution of society the bold, the vigorous, and the buoyant, rise and rule; and that the weak, the shrinking, and the timid, fall and serve." True enough; indisputable, even: but not calculated to appeal to sentimentalists.

In a biographical sketch published in 1963, Norman St. John-Stevas noted Bagehot's unusual capacity to "bridge the gulf between the practical and intellectual worlds." One suspects that Bagehot's upbringing had something to do with this amphibious talent. He was born in Langport, Somerset, to parents whose families dominated the town. Bagehot's father, Thomas—an earnest, pragmatic man—was a partner in the Stuckey Bank, a famous West Country bank that his wife's uncle had founded. (The bank issued its own notes until 1909 and it is said that many Somerset men, suspicious of bank notes issued by a "foreign" London bank, would demand payment in "Stuckeys.") It seems fitting that Walter, who would later join his father in business, was actually born in the bank, in the upstairs living quarters occupied by his parents. Edith Stuckey, ten years Thomas's senior, was a widow when he married her. Of the three children from her first marriage, one was an imbecile and two died in childhood. Walter was the second of two children from her marriage to Thomas, the first of whom also died in childhood. Perhaps in response to these multiple tragedies, Edith Bagehot suffered from periodic bouts of insanity. After her brother died in 1845, Walter became her chief emotional support. As many commentators have noted, the "dark realities" to which he alludes in several essays undoubtedly refer in part to his mother's dementia. "Every trouble in life," he later remarked, "is a joke compared to madness." Despite, or perhaps because of, this mental custodianship, Walter was always extremely close to his mother and was devastated by her death in 1870.

Bagehot's lifelong friend Richard Holt Hutton (1826–1897)—with whom he founded the *National Review* in 1855 and who went on to become editor of the *Spectator*—described Bagehot as "a thorough transcendentalist" but not a "dogmatist." As with many Victorians (and not only Victorians, of course) it is difficult to ascertain all that much about Bagehot's religious convictions. His father, a Unitarian, presided over Sunday morning services at the family house. Walter regularly attended these services—and then accompanied his mother, an ardent Anglican, to the parish church in the afternoon. Bagehot, it is worth remembering, lived at a time when doubt had become an animating principle of faith for many serious people. (As T. S. Eliot said of Tennyson's *In Memoriam* [1850], it is religious not "because of the quality of its faith, but because of the quality of its doubt.") Bagehot flourished just after the time when, as G. M. Young put it in "Portrait of an Age," "one undergraduate has to prepare another undergraduate for the news that a third undergraduate has doubts about the Blessed Trinity." By the time Bagehot came of age, the sea of faith was well advanced on (in Matthew Arnold's famous phrase) its "melancholy, long, withdrawing roar." Whatever the exact nature of Bagehot's doctrinal commitments, he belonged to those determined to preserve the echoes of that retreat, confident, perhaps, that as a tide ebbs so it invariably flows. Alluding to St. Paul, he wrote that

> We know that we see as in a glass darkly; but still we look on the glass. We frame to ourselves some image which we know to be incomplete, which probably is in part untrue, which we try to improve day by day. . . . This is, as it seems, the best religion for finite beings, living, if we may say so, on the very edge of two dissimilar worlds, on the very line on which the infinite, unfathomable sea surges up, and just where the queer little bay of this world ends.

Introduction

In his article on Bagehot for the *Dictionary of National Biography*, Hutton noted that his friend's "great characteristic as a writer, whether on economic or literary subjects, was a very curious combination of dash and doubt, great vivacity in describing the superficial impressions produced on him by every subject-matter with which he was dealing, and great caution in yielding his mind to that superficial impression." This characteristic acted as a prophylactic against dogmatisms of doubt as well as dogmatisms of credulity.

Thomas and Edith Bagehot were both conscientiously solicitous about Walter's education. At thirteen, after grammar school in Langport, he was sent to school in Bristol, where Dr. James Cowles Prichard, Edith's brother-in-law and the founder of the science of anthropology in England, took him under his wing. Prichard's interests made a lasting impression on Walter and echoed in many later works, not least in *Physics and Politics*. University posed a problem. A fervent Nonconformist, Thomas objected to Oxford and Cambridge because of the religious tests that were still in force there. So when he was sixteen, Bagehot went up to University College, London, which had been recently established at the site of a disused garbage dump in Gower Street. Though dogged by ill health—at one point he had to take five months off to recuperate—Bagehot was a brilliant student. He studied mathematics with the eminent, idiosyncratic mathematician Augustus De Morgan, and took a first in classics followed by a first in philosophy and the gold medal in intellectual and moral philosophy. Bagehot met and became friends with R. H. Hutton directly he went up in 1842. In 1848, the year he took his M.A. degree, he met and came under the influence of the poet Arthur Hugh Clough (1819–1861), then principal of University Hall. Clough rather specialized in cultivating intellectual and spiritual impossibilities—Bagehot later criticized his "fatigued way of looking at great subjects"—but, according to Hutton, the poet's adamant negativity exerted a "greater intellectual fascination for Walter Bagehot than any of his contemporaries."

After leaving university in 1848, Bagehot read law. He was called to the bar in 1852, but had by then decided against a legal career and returned to Langport and his father's shipowning and banking business. Banking suited Bagehot. When depressed, he found it cheering to go down to the bank and run his hands through a heap of sovereigns. It was around this time that Bagehot began writing in earnest, contributing literary and biographical articles to *The Prospective Review* and other journals and newspapers. At Clevedon, Somerset, in 1857, he met and was befriended by James Wilson, financial secretary to the Treasury, who had founded *The Economist* in 1843. At the same time he met and befriended Eliza Wilson, the eldest of Wilson's six daughters, a handsome, somewhat neuraesthenic woman who outlived Bagehot by forty-four years. The two soon became engaged and were married the following year. It was an advantageous as well as an affectionate match. At the Wilson's London house in Belgravia, Bagehot met many prominent contemporaries, including Gladstone, Thackeray, Matthew Arnold, and Lord Grey. In 1859, James Wilson went as a financial adviser to India, where he died from dysentery the following year. Meanwhile, he had made Bagehot a director of *The Economist*, which was then being edited by Hutton. After Hutton left to edit the *Spectator*, in 1861, Bagehot took over the editorship of *The Economist*. (The paper was owned by Eliza and her five sisters, who paid him £800 a year for his services.) Bagehot regularly contributed two —and sometimes three or four—articles a week to *The Economist* for the rest of his career.

Bagehot was both intensely social and intensely private. He had, Mrs. Barrington says in her biography, "no enemies but few intimates." Outwardly, the balance of Bagehot's career was uneventful. By all accounts, his childless marriage was extremely happy. He stood for Parliament four times and four times lost, once by seven votes. His always delicate health took a decided turn for the worse in 1867 when he caught pneumonia. He never fully recovered. There followed a succession of chills, colds, and other pulmonary complaints, cheerfully borne but increasingly enervating. In March 1877, Bagehot contracted his last illness: a cold that quickly worsened and within a few days proved fatal. He spent his last hours reading a new copy of Scott's *Rob Roy* (1817) while his wife sat by him, cutting the pages.

It should be noted that Bagehot's magic does not work on everyone. One who is conspicuously resistant to his spell is the English poet and critic C. H. Sisson. In *The Case of Walter Bagehot* (1972), Sisson assembled what amounts to a brief for the prosecution. Sisson's objection to Bagehot is twofold. On the one hand, he sees him as "a founding father of the apologetics of 'fact,'" a skeptical, even cynical, force bent on exploding inherited values. On the other hand, Sisson regards Bagehot as "a moneyed provincial pushing his way in a conventional society." ("Cynical" is a word that often crops up in discussions of Bagehot. Leslie Stephen—in *Studies of a Biographer*—was one of many commentators who discerned a cynical streak in his writing and character, but noted admiringly that "the cynic's merit is to see facts.") "What we get from Bagehot," Mr. Sisson wrote,

> is not so much a theory as a position, and not so much a position as a form of tactics. It is Walter Bagehot whom the successive positions are intended to protect —the Walter Bagehot who slipped down the crack between Unitarianism and Anglicanism; who was the child of the Bank House as some are sons of the manse; whose money was better than that of the squire's but did not produce better effects on the locals; who should have been educated at Oxford but was above that sort of conformism; who conformed instead to the world of business but was cleverer than its other inhabitants; who was all the time worried about the sanity of his stock and did not have any children; who distrusted hereditary powers and owed all his opportunities to family influence.

And so on.

There is probably no antidote to the allergy that Mr. Sisson has to Bagehot. It is the revulsion of one sort of temperament to another that seems antithetical. What Mr. Sisson objects to—a large part of it, anyway—is the very thing that makes Bagehot Bagehot. Not his subtlety, exactly, but his deployment of subtlety. Bagehot seldom runs on one track. Whatever topic he is pursuing, he habitually manages to look behind it as well. It is not irony, precisely, for although he *uses* irony, Bagehot is too earnest to be described as ironical.

The same goes for "cynicism." Bagehot could be sharp; he could be startling; he could be dismissive; but he was

too aware of possibility to rest in cynicism. Jacques Barzun referred in this context to Bagehot's "binocular vision," his habit of taking "double views." The historian
Gertrude Himmelfarb, in "Walter Bagehot: A Common
Man with Uncommon Ideas," observes that "he was that
rare species of the twice-born who could give proper due
to the rights and merits of the once-born. And he did so
not by a denial of his own nature but by virtue of the very
subtleties, complications, and ambiguities that informed
his nature."

What another critic has dubbed Bagehot's "duomania"
shows itself even in his methods of analysis. Bagehot is
fond—perhaps overly fond—of breaking his subjects into
two categories. When he talks about genius, he begins by
discerning two types, regular and irregular; religion
comes in two flavors, natural and supernatural; biography is selective or it is exhaustive; fiction is either ubi-
quitous or sentimental; goodness is sensuous or ascetic.
Writers, he says, like teeth, "are divided into incisors and
grinders." A rare exception to this law of pairs is found in
Bagehot's famous essay on Wordsworth, Tennyson, and
Browning (1864), which unfolds a tripart division of
"Pure, Ornate, and Grotesque Art in English Poetry."

In fact, the duality one sees in Bagehot's work reflects
a duality in his character. On the one hand, we have
Bagehot the apostle of "dullness," extolling stolidness in
individuals and governments alike. On the other hand, we
find him (in an essay on the eighteenth-century wit Lady
Mary Wortley Montagu) noting how easy it is to dull the
mind "by a vapid accumulation of torpid comfort."

Many of the middle classes spend their whole lives in a
constant series of petty pleasures, and an undeviating

pursuit of small material objects. The gross pursuit of pleasure, and the tiresome pursuit of petty comfort, are quite suitable to such "a being as man in such a world as the present one." What is not possible is to combine the pursuit of pleasure and the enjoyment of comfort with the characteristic pleasures of a strong mind. If you wish for luxury, you must not nourish the inquisitive instinct.

Again, we have Bagehot the banker and man of affairs—the man St. John-Stevas describes as "a sardonic, no-nonsense, experienced man of the world," and, opposing him, we have "the passionate, mystical Bagehot" who understands that what really matters in life is not calculable in terms of a profit-and-loss ledger. "No real Englishman, in his secret soul," Bagehot observed, "was ever sorry for the death of a political economist: he is much more likely to be sorry for his life." The "mystical" side of Bagehot peeks out most conspicuously in some of his literary essays. In "The First Edinburgh Reviewers" (1855), one of his most celebrated essays, Bagehot writes that "a clear, precise, discriminating intellect shrinks at once from the symbolic, the unbounded, the indefinite." He then goes on—it is the quintessential Bagehot touch— to observe that "the misfortune is that mysticism is true."

There are certainly kinds of truth, borne in as it were instinctively on the human intellect, most influential on the character and heart, yet hardly capable of stringent definition. Their course is shadowy; the mind seems rather to have seen than to see them, more to feel after than definitely apprehend them. They commonly involve an infinite element, which of course cannot be stated precisely, or else a first principle—an original tendency—of our intellectual constitution, which it is impossible not to feel, and yet which it is hard to extricate in terms and words.

The real motor for Bagehot's "duality" was his inextinguishable sense of the incongruous. "How can a soul be a merchant?" he asks. "What relation to an immortal being have the price of linseed, the fall of butter, the tare on tallow, or the brokerage on hemp? Can an undying creature debit *petty expense* and charge for *carriage paid*? . . . The soul ties its shoe; the mind washes its hands in a basin. All is incongruous." One of the things that makes Bagehot's writing so tonic is his refusal to resolve such incongruities. A more pedestrian writer, contemplating the absurdity of the soul tying its shoe, would dispense with the soul and come down firmly on the side of the footwear. It is part of Bagehot's genius to preserve the extravagance—not because it is startling but because it is true to our experience of the world.

Bagehot's greatest achievement was in applying his "binocular vision," his incorrigible sense of the incongruous, to the realm of politics and social life. His talents in this regard were already fully developed in the seven letters that he wrote about Louis Napoleon's *coup d'état* for *The Inquirer*, a Unitarian paper of abundant goodwill and characteristic shallowness. Bagehot was only twenty-five in December 1851 when the *coup* began. But the letters show that he was already a master of controversy and in full possession of several themes that would occupy him later.

Bagehot certainly knew how to get his readers' attention. Noting that "the first duty of a government is to ensure the security of that industry which is the condition of social life," he went on cheerfully to defend Louis's use of force and approve his curtailing the French press. The effect of Louis's intervention, Bagehot wrote, "was magical. . . . Commerce instantly improved," the boulevards were once again "gay and splendid; people began again to buy, and consequently to sell." Not that Bagehot was surprised by Louis Napoleon's appeal; after all, he was bold; he had "never been a professor, nor a journalist, nor a promising barrister, nor, by taste, a *littérateur.*"

These were powerful, if negative, recommendations for leadership in Bagehot's view. Besides, the French people had time and again shown that they were too clever to be trusted with political liberty. "With a well-balanced national character," Bagehot argued, "liberty is a stable thing." "Stupidity," he wrote in a famous passage, is "about the most essential mental quality for a free people, whose liberty is to be progressive, permanent, and on a large scale." Stupidity was "nature's favorite recourse for preserving steadiness of conduct and consistency of opinion." But a Frenchman, according to Bagehot, is constitutionally incapable of stupidity: "*esprit* is his essence, wit is to him as water, *bon-mots* as *bon-bons.*" Liberty is pleasant; but "the best institutions will not keep right a nation that *will* go wrong."

ALL THIS, of course, outraged the good readers of *The Inquirer*, who detested Louis Napoleon, were aghast at his dictatorial pretensions, and regarded any infringement on British-style liberty (at least in Europe) as unconscionable. Then, too, there was the embarrassing syllogism that if "stupidity" was a prerequisite for political freedom, and if the English were peculiarly suited for liberty, then the English must be mired in stupidity. Well, Bagehot would not have said "mired." But he claimed early and often that stupidity was an Englishman's birthright. "A great part of the 'best' English people," he wrote in *The English Constitution*, "keep their mind in a state of decorous dullness. They maintain their dignity; they get obeyed; they are good and charitable to their dependents. But they have no notion of *play* of mind; no conception that the charm of society depends upon it." Even worse, perhaps, than Bagehot's praise of stupidity and dullness were the kind things he found to say about the reactionary behavior of the French Catholic Church, an unpardonable abomination to many of his readers. "Tell an Englishman that a building is without use and he will stare," Bagehot wrote elsewhere; "that it is illiberal, and he will survey it; that it teaches Aristotle, and he will seem perplexed; that it don't teach science, and he won't mind; but only hint that it is the Pope, and he will arise and burn it to the ground."

Naturally, a good deal of Bagehot's outrageousness in his missives to *The Inquirer* was calculated; but this was small comfort to its owners, who found that his contributions almost ruined the paper. The sober backdrop to Bagehot's rhetoric was the Burkean theme that stresses the importance of "sense and circumstance" in politics. Above all, Bagehot was writing against "the old idea which still here creeps out in conversation, and sometimes in writing," that

> politics are simply a subdivision of immutable ethics; that there are certain rights of men in all places and all times, which are the sole and sufficient foundation of all government, and that accordingly a single stereo-

type government is to make the tour of the world—and you have no more right to deprive a Dyak of his vote in a "possible" Polynesian Parliament, than you have to steal his mat.

Here again, we see that the pertinence of Bagehot's political reflections is by no means limited to the nineteenth century.

The difficult insight that Bagehot is everywhere at pains to communicate is that not all things are possible at all times and all places. If political liberty is a precious possession, it is forged in a long, painful development of civilization, much of which is distinctly, and necessarily, illiberal. Hence the advantage of binocular vision, which allowed Bagehot, even as he was extolling Louis Napoleon's *coup*, to risk his life helping the republicans build barricades. This was not an expression of irony or inconstancy on Bagehot's part; it was an expression of political realism. As he put it later in "Caesarism as It Now Exists" (1865), the Second Empire was "an admirable government for present and coarse purposes, but a detestable government for future and refined purposes." One can help prepare for the future; one must live in the present.

The ideas that found preliminary expression in Bagehot's letters on Louis Napoleon's *coup* recur again and again in his writings. They received their most complete development in *Physics and Politics*. Of the six essays that compose the book, five were serialized in the *Fortnightly Review* beginning in 1867. A bad bout of pneumonia interrupted his work, but Bagehot added the final essay, "Verifiable Progress Politically Considered," when he published the book version in 1872.

The notion that human beings—and, by analogy, that advanced human societies—had developed out of more primitive forms had been in the air for decades by the time Bagehot began *Physics and Politics*. Evolution—often called "descent with modification" or simply "development" in the early nineteenth century—was, as the philosopher David Stove pointed out in *Darwinian Fairytales*, an Enlightenment idea par excellence. Darwin's theories about the place of natural selection in biological evolution, published in 1859 in *On the Origin of Species*, gave the idea of evolution new scientific authority. But the basic idea of evolution—minus the explanatory motor of natural selection, which Darwin adopted from Thomas Malthus's *Essay on Population* (first published in 1798) —was part of the mental furniture of the age. Robert Chambers's *Vestiges of the Natural History of Creation*, published in 1844, was one of several books on the subject that influenced Bagehot. The crudities of "Social Darwinism," put forward most famously in the writings and speeches of Herbert Spencer (1820–1903) and T. H. Huxley (1825–1895), were a natural outgrowth of these ideas. (Huxley earned the sobriquet "Darwin's bulldog" for his tireless advocacy of Darwinism.)

The long subtitle of *Physics and Politics*—"Thoughts on the Application of the Principles of 'Natural Selection' and 'Inheritance' to Political Society"—certainly suggests that it belongs to that unpromising genre of muscular Darwinism. As always with Bagehot, however, things are not as straightforward as they at first seem. To be sure, by "physics" Bagehot meant "science," more particularly "Darwinism." (Perhaps a more accurate title would have been *Biology and Politics*, though doubtless Bagehot had in mind the etymology of "physics," i.e., "nature.") He approvingly quoted various works by Spencer and Huxley, and indeed such passages are among the most dated in the book. He referred on and off to the "transmitted nerve element" and other Lamarckian museum pieces. (Gregor Mendel's discoveries in what we have come to call genetics were published in 1866 but remained unrecognized until this century.)

THE POINT to bear in mind is that Bagehot early on made it clear that in invoking the idea of natural selection he was merely "searching out and following up an analogy." As Crane Brinton put it in his chapter on "The Prosperous Victorians" in *English Political Thought in the Nineteenth Century*, Bagehot "is never dogmatic, never desirous of proving too much, even to himself. He merely examines, with due regard for the limitations of logic, some of the implications of the doctrine of the survival of the fittest applied to human society. He is concerned with the nature and survival of what common sense calls a 'national character,' and which exists for every group." The great theme of *Physics and Politics*, Bagehot writes in his last chapter, concerns "the political prerequisites of progress, and especially of early progress." Just how far Bagehot's use of the term "natural selection" is from Darwin's stricter signification is shown by the way he links its operation to the operation of Providence—an agency conspicuously missing from any orthodox Darwinian account of evolution. "By a law of which we know no reason," Bagehot notes, "but which is among the first by which Providence guides and governs the world, there is a tendency in descendants to be like their progenitors, and yet a tendency also in descendants to *differ* from their progenitors. The work of nature in making generations is a patchwork—part resemblance, part contrast."

As usual, Bagehot has two main ideas. The first concerns the enormous difficulty our forefathers must have faced in establishing *any* political order or rule of law, benevolent or otherwise:

> In early times the quantity of government is much more important than its quality. What you want is a comprehensive rule binding men together, . . . What this rule is does not matter so much. A good rule is better than a bad one, but any rule is better than none; while, for reasons which a jurist will appreciate, none can be very good. But to gain that rule, what may be called the impressive elements of a polity are incomparably more important than its useful elements. How to get the obedience of men is the hard problem; what you do with that obedience is less critical.

Bagehot's second idea concerns the similarly difficult task later ages always face in advancing beyond the order that made their own existence possible. The first step—inaugurating law, custom, and habit—is the hardest; but history proper begins with the next step: "What is most evident is not the difficulty of getting fixed law, but getting out of a fixed law; not of cementing . . . a cake of custom, but of breaking the cake of custom; not of making the first preservative habit, but of breaking through it, and reaching something better." In his second chapter, "The Use of Conflict," he sums up the "the strict dilemma of early society."

Either men had no law at all, and lived in confused

tribes, hardly hanging together, or they had to obtain a fixed law by processes of incredible difficulty. Those who surmounted that difficulty soon destroyed all those that lay in their way who did not. And then they themselves were caught in their own yoke. The customary discipline, which could only be imposed on any early men by terrible sanctions, continued with those sanctions, and killed out of the whole society the propensities to variation which are the principle of progress.

Experience shows how incredibly difficult it is to get men really to encourage the principle of originality. They will admit it in theory, but in practice the old error—the error which arrested a hundred civilizations—returns again. Men are too fond of their own life, too credulous of the completeness of their own ideas, too angry at the pain of new thoughts, to be able to bear easily with a changing existence; or else, *having* new ideas, they want to enforce them on mankind—to make them heard, and admitted, and obeyed before, in simple competition with other ideas, they would ever be so naturally. At this very moment there are the most rigid Comtists teaching that we ought to be governed by a hierarchy—a combination of savants orthodox in science. Yet who can doubt that Comte would have been hanged by his own hierarchy?

Bagehot traces the vicissitudes of this dialectic through various stages from "The Preliminary Age"—that is, the rude time of prehistory when (he says with some exaggeration) "the strongest killed out the weakest as they could"—to modern times and "The Age of Discussion." Along the way Bagehot discusses the civilizing—or at least order-inducing—effects of violence ("The Use of Conflict") and the hard road any population faces in forging a national identity ("Nation-making"). The perennial problem—and the admonitory theme of *Physics and Politics*—is that man, the strongest and smartest of the animals, "was obliged to be his own domesticator; he had to tame himself." Consequently, "history is strewn with the wrecks of nations which have gained a little progressiveness at the cost of a great deal of hard manliness, and have thus prepared themselves for destruction as soon as the movements of the world gave a chance for it."

There is a great deal in *Physics and Politics* to shock readers inclined to a pacific view of human development or a politically correct understanding of life. About philanthropy in general, Bagehot shared the suspicions of many nineteenth-century conservatives:

The most melancholy of human reflections, perhaps, is that, on the whole, it is a question whether the benevolence of mankind does most good or harm. Great good, no doubt, philanthropy does, but then it also does great evil. It augments so much vice, it multiplies so much suffering, it brings to life such great populations to suffer and to be vicious, that it is open to argument whether it be or be not an evil to the world, and this is entirely because excellent people fancy they can do much by rapid action—that they will most benefit the world when they most relieve their own feelings.

Bagehot was even more controversial in other areas. "Let us consider," he writes in a famous passage toward the end of *Physics and Politics*, in what sense a village of English colonists is superior to a tribe of Australian natives who roam about them. Indisputably in one, and that a main sense, they are superior. They can beat the Australians in war when they like; they can take from them anything they like, and kill any of them they choose. As a rule, in all the outlying and uncontested districts of the world, the aboriginal native lies at the mercy of the intruding European. Nor is this all. Indisputably in the English village there are more means of happiness, a greater accumulation of the instruments of enjoyment, than in the Australian tribe. The English have all manner of books, utensils, and machines which the others do not use, value, or understand. And in addition . . . there is a general strength which is capable of being used in conquering a thousand difficulties, and is an abiding source of happiness.

In fact, the importance of military prowess in binding a population into a society is a leitmotif in *Physics and Politics*. In "The Use of Conflict," Bagehot notes that the progress of the military art is the "most conspicuous, I was about to say the most *showy*," fact in human history. "All through the earliest times," he writes,

> martial merit is a token of real merit: the nation that wins is the nation that ought to win. The simple virtues of such ages mostly make a man a soldier if they make him anything. No doubt the brute force of number may be too potent even then (as so often it is afterwards): civilization may be thrown back by the conquest of many very rude men over a few less rude men. But the first elements of civilization are great military

advantages, and, roughly, it is a rule of the first times that you can infer merit from conquest, and that progress is promoted by the competitive examination of constant war.

Bagehot is undeceived about exigencies that face a nation at war. "So long as war is the main business of nations, temporary despotism—despotism during the campaign—is indispensable. Macaulay justly said that many an army has prospered under a bad commander, but no army has ever prospered under a 'debating society.'"

The point is, Bagehot argues, that "war both needs and generates certain virtues; not the highest, but what may be called the preliminary virtues, as valor, veracity, the spirit of obedience, the habit of discipline." That is to say, war, and the martial virtues it requires, makes certain valuable things possible, including civilization itself: "Civilization begins," Bagehot writes, "because the beginning of civilization is a military advantage"—an unflattering thought that many will find shocking.

Even more shocking is the similar argument that Bagehot makes regarding slavery:

Slavery, too, has a bad name in the later world, and very justly. We connect it with gangs in chains, with laws which keep men ignorant, with laws that hinder families. But the evils which we have endured from slavery in recent ages must not blind us to, or make us forget, the great services that slavery rendered in early ages. . . . Refinement is only possible when leisure is possible; and slavery first makes it possible.

Perhaps the only thing more difficult than accepting this

contention is coming up with convincing arguments against it.

All such "hard" observations constitute as it were the strophe of Bagehot's argument. The antistrophe, the opposite movement—the movement toward which *Physics and Politics* as a whole tends—is that "the whole history of civilization is strewn with creeds and institutions which were invaluable at first, and deadly afterwards." Slavery is one such institution. And ultimately the martial sensibility may be as well.

> Life is not a set campaign, but an irregular work, and the main forces in it are not overt resolutions, but latent and half-involuntary promptings. The mistake of military ethics is to exaggerate the conception of discipline, and so to present the moral force of the will in a barer form than it ever ought to take. Military morals can direct the axe to cut down the tree, but it knows nothing of the quiet force by which the forest grows.

Savages, Bagehot writes with cool dispatch, prefer "short spasms of greedy pleasure to mild and equable enjoyment." Thus it is that progress in civilization is measured by increasing deliberateness. Government—the institutional distillate of progress in civilization—is valuable not only because it facilitates action but also, and increasingly, because it retards it:

> If you want to stop instant and immediate action, always make it a condition that the action shall not begin till a considerable number of persons have talked over it, and have agreed on it. If those persons be

people of different temperaments, different ideas, and different educations, you have an almost infallible security that nothing, or almost nothing, will be done with excessive rapidity.

It is naturally "the age of discussion"—the age of "slow" government and political liberty—that Bagehot ultimately extols in *Physics and Politics*. But Bagehot is ever at pains to remind his readers of the harsh prerequisites of civilization, which include war, slavery, and gross inequity. Government by discussion, Bagehot is quick to acknowledge, is "a principal organ for improving mankind." At the same time, he insists that "it is a plant of singular delicacy." The question of how best to nurture this delicate plant is Bagehot's final problem. Part of the answer is in facing up to the unpalatable realities about power that make civilization possible. The other part lies in embracing what Bagehot calls "animated moderation," that "union of life with measure, of spirit with reasonableness," which assures that discussion will continue without descending into violence or anarchy. It seems like a small thing. But then achieved order always does—until it is lost.

RK January 1999

Acknowledgments

I have benefitted greatly from the advice, editorial scrutiny, and miscellaneous assistance of several people in the preparation of this edition of *Physics and Politics*. At *The New Criterion*, I would like to mention in particular Hilton Kramer, who first introduced me to Bagehot's work and early on encouraged me in this project. I am also grateful to my colleagues Sara Lussier and Robert Messenger. Sir Hugh Lloyd-Jones read and made valuable suggestions about an earlier version of the introduction, and John Gross generously read and commented on the introduction and notes. I am also grateful to my publisher, Ivan R. Dee, for cheerfully undertaking this worthy though commercially adventurous project. My largest debt is to Alexandra Kimball, who devoted many hours to helping me track down some difficult-to-find references, who prepared the index, and who otherwise helped in tidying up the text for publication.

Note on the Text

P *hysics and Politics* was first published in book form in 1872 by Henry S. King of London in its International Scientific Series. Of the six essays that compose the book, the first five were serialized in the *Fortnightly Review*. The first appeared in November 1867, the second in April 1868, the third in July 1869, the fourth in December 1871, and the fifth in January 1872. Bagehot wrote the brief concluding essay for the book version. As he notes at the beginning of that last essay, the long delays were due to recurring ill health. There are numerous small differences between the essays as they originally appeared in the *Fortnightly Review* and the book version, all of which are noted in Norman St. John-Stevas's edition of *Physics and Politics*, which appears in Volume VII of *The Collected Works of Walter Bagehot* (London: The Economist, 1974). In the present edition, I have generally followed St. John-Stevas, though I have also compared the text to the edition edited by Jacques Barzun in 1948. Barzun silently modernized Bagehot's punctuation and Americanized some of his spelling; I have followed his example, further modernizing the text and silently correcting a small number of typographical errors. Bagehot refers to a wide range of literary, scientific, and scholarly figures, many of whom will be unfamiliar to most contemporary readers. I have identified all but the most well known and have given references for works that Bagehot quotes at length. Bagehot's few notes are indicated by an asterisk. The editor's notes are further distinguished by square brackets and the designation "—*Ed.*"

Physics and Politics

1

The Preliminary Age

I

O NE peculiarity of this age is the sudden acquisition of much physical knowledge. There is scarcely a department of science or art which is the same, or at all the same, as it was fifty years ago. A new world of inventions—of railways and of telegraphs—has grown up around us which we cannot help seeing; a new world of ideas is in the air and affects us, though we do not see it. A full estimate of these effects would require a great book, and I am sure I could not write it; but I think I may usefully, in a few papers, show how, upon one or two great points, the new ideas are modifying two old sciences—politics and political economy. Even upon these points my ideas must be incomplete, for the subject is novel; but, at any rate, I may suggest some conclusions and so show what is requisite even if I do not supply it.

If we wanted to describe one of the most marked results, perhaps the most marked result, of late thought, we should say that by it everything is made "an antiquity." When, in former times, our ancestors thought of an antiquarian, they described him as occupied with coins, and medals, and Druids' stones; these were then the characteristic records of the decipherable past, and it was with these that decipherers busied themselves. But now there are other relics; indeed, all matter is become such. Science tries to find in each bit of earth the record of the causes which made it precisely what it is; those forces have left their trace, she knows, as much as the tact and hand of the artist left their mark on a classical gem. It would be tedious (and it is not in my way) to reckon up the ingenious questionings by which geology has made part of the earth, at least, tell part of its tale; and the answers would have been meaningless if physiology and conchology and a hundred similar sciences had not brought their aid. Such subsidiary sciences are to the decipherer of the present day what old languages were to the antiquary of other days; they construe for him the words which he discovers, they give a richness and a truth-like complexity to the picture which he paints, even in cases where the particular detail they tell is not much. But what here concerns me is that man himself has, to the eye of science, become "an antiquity." She tries to read, is beginning to read, knows she ought to read, in the frame of each man the result of a whole history of all his life, of what he is and what makes him so—of all his forefathers, of what they were and of what made them so. Each nerve has a sort of memory of its past life, is trained or not trained, dulled or quickened, as the case may be; each feature is shaped and characterized, or left loose and meaningless, as may happen; each hand is marked with its trade and life, subdued to what it works in—*if we could but see it.*

It may be answered that in this there is nothing new; that we always knew how much a man's past modified a man's future; that we all knew how much a man is apt to be like his ancestors; that the existence of national character is the greatest commonplace in the world; that when a philosopher cannot account for anything in any other manner, he boldly ascribes it to an occult quality in some race. But what physical science does is, not to discover the hereditary element, but to render it distinct—to give us an accurate conception of what we may expect, and a good account of the evidence by which we are led to expect it. Let us see what that science teaches on the subject; and, as far as may be, I will give it in the words of those who have made it a professional study, both that I may be more sure to state it rightly and vividly, and because—as I am about to apply these principles to subjects which are my own pursuit—I would rather have it quite clear that I have not made my premises to suit my own conclusions.

First, then, as respects the individual, we learn as follows:

Even while the cerebral hemispheres are entire, and in full possession of their powers, the brain gives rise to actions which are as completely reflex as those of the spinal cord.

When the eyelids wink at a flash of light, or a threatened blow, a reflex action takes place, in which the afferent nerves are the optic, the efferent, the facial. When a bad smell causes a grimace, there is a reflex action through the same motor nerve, while the olfactory nerves constitute the afferent channels. In these cases, therefore, reflex action must be effected through the brain, all the nerves involved being cerebral.

When the whole body starts at a loud noise, the afferent auditory nerve gives rise to an impulse which passes to the medulla oblongata, and thence affects the great majority of the motor nerves of the body.

It may be said that these are mere mechanical actions, and have nothing to do with the acts which we associate with intelligence. But let us consider what takes place in such an act as reading aloud. In this case, the whole attention of the mind is, or ought to be, bent upon the subject-matter of the book; while a multitude of most delicate muscular actions are going on, of which the reader is not in the slightest degree aware. Thus the book is held in the hand, at the right distance from the eyes; the eyes are moved, from side to side, over the lines, and up and down the pages. Further, the most delicately adjusted and rapid movements of the muscles of the lips, tongue, and throat, of laryngeal and respiratory muscles, are involved in the production of speech. Perhaps the reader is standing up and accompanying the lecture with appropriate gestures. And yet every one of these muscular acts may be performed with utter unconsciousness, on his part, of anything but the sense of the words in the book. In other words, they are reflex acts.

The reflex actions proper to the spinal cord itself are *natural*, and are involved in the structure of the cord and the properties of its constituents. By the help of the brain we may acquire an affinity of *artificial* reflex actions. That is to say, an action may require all our attention and all our volition for its first, or second, or third performance, but by frequent repetition it becomes, in a manner, part of our organization, and is performed without volition, or even consciousness.

As everyone knows, it takes a soldier a very long time to learn his drill—to put himself, for instance, into the attitude of "attention" at the instant the word of command is heard. But, after a time, the sound of the word gives rise to the act, whether the soldier be thinking of it or not. There is a story, which is credible enough, though it may not be true, of a practical joker, who, seeing a discharged veteran carrying home his dinner, suddenly called out "Attention!" whereupon the man instantly brought his hands down, and lost his mutton and potatoes in the gutter. The drill had been gone through, and its effects had become embodied in the man's nervous structure.

The possibility of all education (of which military drill is only one particular form) is based upon the existence of this power which the nervous system possesses, of organizing conscious actions into more or less unconscious, or reflex, operations. It may be laid down as a rule, that if any two mental states be called up together, or in succession, with due frequency and vividness, the subsequent production of the one of them will suffice to call up the other, and that whether we desire it or not.*

The body of the accomplished man has thus become by training different from what it once was, and different from that of the rude man; it is charged with stored vir-

* Huxley's *Elementary Physiology*, pages 284–286. [T(homas) H(enry) Huxley (1825–1895), grandfather of the novelist Aldous Huxley, was a natural historian and popular lecturer. His enthusiastic proselytizing of behalf Darwin's theory of evolution by natural selection earned him the nickname "Darwin's bulldog." The book from which Bagehot quotes is *Lessons in Elementary Physiology* (London: Macmillan, 1866).—Ed.]

tue and acquired faculty which come away from it unconsciously.

Again, as to race, another authority teaches:

Man's life truly represents a progressive development of the nervous system, none the less so because it takes place out of the womb instead of in it. The regular transmutation of motions which are at first voluntary into secondary automatic motions, as Hartley calls them, is due to a gradually effected organization; and we may rest assured of this, that coordinate activity always testifies to stored-up power, either innate or acquired.

The way in which an acquired faculty of the parent animal is sometimes distinctly transmitted to the progeny as a heritage, instinct, or innate endowment, furnishes a striking confirmation of the foregoing observations. Power that has been laboriously acquired and stored up as statical in one generation manifestly in such case becomes the inborn faculty of the next; and the development takes place in accordance with that law of increasing speciality and complexity of adaptation to external nature which is traceable through the animal kingdom, or, in other words, that law of progress from the general to the special in development which the appearance of nerve force amongst natural forces and the complexity of the nervous system of man both illustrate. As the vital force gathers up, as it were, into itself inferior forces, and might be said to be a development of them, or, as in the appearance of nerve force, simpler and more general forces are gathered up and concentrated in a more special and complex mode of energy; so again a further specialization takes place in the development of the nervous system, whether watched through generations or through individual life. It is not by limiting our observations to the life of the individual, however, who is but a link in the chain of organic beings connecting the past with the future, that we shall come at the full truth; the present individual is the inevitable consequence of his antecedents in the past, and in the examination of these alone do we arrive at the adequate explanation of him. It behooves us, then, having found any faculty to be innate, not to rest content there, but steadily to follow backwards the line of causation, and thus to display, if possible, its manner of origin. This is the more necessary with the lower animals, where so much is innate.*

The special laws of inheritance are indeed as yet unknown. All which is clear, and all which is to my purpose, is that there is a tendency, a probability, greater or less according to circumstances, but always considerable, that the descendants of cultivated parents will have, by born nervous organization, a greater aptitude for cultivation than the descendants of such as are not cultivated; and that this tendency augments, in some enhanced ratio, for many generations.

* Maudsley on the *Physiology and Pathology of the Mind*, page 73. [Henry Maudsley (1835–1918) was an important English doctor and philanthropist. A facsimile of the work that Bagehot quotes, a nineteenth-century classic, is reprinted in *Significant Contributions to the History of Psychology, 1750–1920*, edited and with a preface by Daniel Robinson (Washington, D.C.: University Publications of America, Inc., 1977).—Ed.]

I do not think any who do not acquire—and it takes a hard effort to acquire—this notion of a transmitted nerve element will ever understand "the connective tissue" of civilization. We have here the continuous force which binds age to age, which enables each to begin with some improvement on the last, if the last did itself improve; which makes each civilization not a set of detached dots, but a line of color, surely enhancing shade by shade. There is, by this doctrine, a physical cause of improvement from generation to generation: and no imagination which has apprehended it can forget it; but unless you appreciate that cause in its subtle materialism, unless you see it, as it were, playing upon the nerves of men, and, age after age, making nicer music from finer chords, you cannot comprehend the principle of inheritance either in its mystery or its power.

These principles are quite independent of any theory as to the nature of matter, or the nature of mind. They are as true upon the theory that mind acts on matter—though separate and altogether different from it—as upon the theory of Bishop Berkeley that there is no matter, but only mind; or upon the contrary theory—that there is no mind, but only matter; or upon the yet subtler theory now often held—that both mind and matter are different modifications of some one *tertium quid*, some hidden thing or force. All these theories admit—indeed, they are but various theories to account for—the fact that what we call matter has consequences in what we call mind; and that what we call mind produces results in what we call matter; and the doctrines I quote assume only that. Our mind in some strange way acts on our nerves, and our nerves in some equally strange way store up the consequences, and somehow the result, as a rule and commonly enough, goes down to our descendants; these primitive facts all theories admit, and all of them labor to explain.

Nor have these plain principles any relation to the old difficulties of necessity and free will. Every free-willist holds that the special force of free volition is applied to the pre-existing forces of our corporeal structure; he does not consider it as an agency acting *in vacuo*, but as an agency acting upon other agencies. Every free-willist holds that, upon the whole, if you strengthen the motive in a given direction, mankind tend more to act in that direction. Better motives—better impulses, rather come from a good body: worse motives or worse impulses come from a bad body. A free-willist may admit as much as a necessarian that such improved conditions tend to improve human action, and that deteriorated conditions tend to deprave human action. No free-willist ever expects as much from St. Giles's as he expects from Belgravia: he admits an hereditary nervous system as a *datum* for the will, though he holds the will to be an extraordinary incoming "something." No doubt the modern doctrine of the "Conservation of Force," if applied to decision, is inconsistent with free will; if you hold that force "is never lost or gained," you cannot hold that there is a real gain—a sort of new creation of it in free volition. But I have nothing to do here with the universal "Conservation of Force." The conception of the nervous organs as stores of will-made power does not raise or need so vast a discussion.

Still less are these principles to be confounded with Mr. Buckle's* idea that material forces have been the main-

---

* [Henry Thomas Buckle (1821–1862), a radical free-thinker and self-taught historian. His *History of Civilization in*

springs of progress, and moral causes secondary, and, in comparison, not to be thought of. On the contrary, moral causes are the first here. It is the action of the will that causes the unconscious habit; it is the continual effort of the beginning that creates the hoarded energy of the end; it is the silent toil of the first generation that becomes the transmitted aptitude of the next. Here physical causes do not create the moral, but moral create the physical; here the beginning is by the higher energy, the conservation and propagation only by the lower. But we thus perceive how a science of history is possible, as Mr. Buckle said—a science to teach the laws of tendencies—created by the mind, and transmitted by the body—which act upon and incline the will of man from age to age.

II

But how do these principles change the philosophy of our politics? I think in many ways; and first, in one particularly. Political economy is the most systematized and most accurate part of political philosophy; and yet, by the help of what has been laid down, I think we may travel back to a sort of "pre-economic age," when the very assumptions of political economy did not exist, when its precepts would have been ruinous, and when the very contrary precepts were requisite and wise.

For this purpose I do not need to deal with the dim ages which ethnology just reveals to us—with the stone

---

England (first volume, 1857, second volume 1861)—a book much admired by Darwin—sought to uncover unchanging natural laws to explain historical development.—*Ed.*]

age, and the flint implements, and the refuse heaps. The time to which I would go back is only that just before the dawn of history—coeval with the dawn, perhaps, it would be right to say—for the first historians saw such a state of society, though they saw other and more advanced states too: a period of which we have distinct descriptions from eye-witnesses, and of which the traces and consequences abound in the oldest law. "The effect," says Sir Henry Maine, the greatest of our living jurists—the only one, perhaps, whose writings are in keeping with our best philosophy—"of the evidence derived from comparative jurisprudence is to establish that view of the primeval condition of the human race which is known as the Patriarchal Theory."*

There is no doubt, of course, that this theory was originally based on the Scriptural history of the Hebrew patriarchs in Lower Asia; but, as has been explained already, its connection with Scripture rather militated than otherwise against its reception as a complete theory, since the majority of the inquirers who till recently addressed themselves with most earnestness to the colligation of social phenomena, were either influenced by the strongest prejudice against Hebrew antiquities or by the strongest desire to con-

---

* [The work of Sir Henry Maine (1822–1888), English jurist and historian, greatly influenced Bagehot. Especially important was *Ancient Law: Its Connection with the Early History of Society, and Its Relation to Modern Ideas* (1861), a classic of legal history. The following quotation comes from Chapter Five, "Primitive and Ancient Law," pages 199–120. —Ed.]

struct their system without the assistance of religious records. Even now there is perhaps a disposition to undervalue these accounts, or rather to decline generalizing from them, as forming part of the traditions of a Semitic people. It is to be noted, however, that the legal testimony comes nearly exclusively from the institutions of societies belonging to the Indo-European stock, the Romans, Hindoos, and Sclavonians supplying the greater part of it; and indeed the difficulty, at the present stage of the inquiry, is to know where to stop, to say of what races of men it is *not* allowable to lay down that the society in which they are united was originally organized on the patriarchal model. The chief lineaments of such a society, as collected from the early chapters in Genesis, I need not attempt to depict with any minuteness, both because they are familiar to most of us from our earliest childhood, and because, from the interest once attaching to the controversy which takes its name from the debate between Locke and Filmer, they fill a whole chapter, though not a very profitable one, in English literature. The points which lie on the surface of the history are these:—The eldest male parent—the eldest ascendant—is absolutely supreme in his household. His dominion extends to life and death, and is as unqualified over his children and their houses as over his slaves; indeed the relations of sonship and serfdom appear to differ in little beyond the higher capacity which the child in blood possesses of becoming one day the head of a family himself. The flocks and herds of the children are the flocks and herds of the father, and the possessions of the parent, which he holds in a representative rather than in a proprietary character, are equally divided at his death among his descendants in the first degree, the eldest son sometimes receiving a double share under the name of birthright, but more generally endowed with no hereditary advantage beyond an honorary precedence. A less obvious inference from the Scriptural accounts is that they seem to plant us on the traces of the breach which is first effected in the empire of the parent. The families of Jacob and Esau separate and form two nations; but the families of Jacob's children hold together and become a people. This looks like the immature germ of a state or commonwealth, and of an order of rights superior to the claims of family relation.

If I were attempting for the more special purposes of the jurist to express compendiously the characteristics of the situation in which mankind disclose themselves at the dawn of their history, I should be satisfied to quote a few verses from the *Odyssey* of Homer:

τοῖσιν δ᾽ οὔτ᾽ ἀγοραὶ βουληφόροι οὔτε θέμιστες, . . .
θεμιστεύει δὲ ἕκαστος
παίδων ἠδ᾽ ἀλόχων, οὐδ᾽ ἀλλήλων ἀλέγουσιν.

"They have neither assemblies for consultation nor *themistes*, but everyone exercises jurisdiction over his wives and his children, and they pay no regard to one another."*

And this description of the beginnings of history is confirmed by what may be called the last lesson of pre-

---

* [*Odyssey* IX:112ff.—*Ed.*]

historic ethnology. Perhaps it is the most valuable, as it is clearly the most sure result of that science, that it has dispelled the dreams of other days as to a primitive high civilization. History catches man as he emerges from the patriarchal state: ethnology shows how he lived, grew, and improved in that state. The conclusive arguments against the imagined original civilization are indeed plain to everyone. Nothing is more intelligible than a moral deterioration of mankind—nothing than an aesthetic degradation—nothing than a political degradation. But you cannot imagine mankind giving up the plain utensils of personal comfort, if they once knew them; still less can you imagine them giving up good weapons—say bows and arrows—if they once knew them. Yet if there were a primitive civilization these things *must* have been forgotten, for tribes can be found in every degree of ignorance, and every grade of knowledge as to pottery, as to the metals, as to the means of comfort, as to the instruments of war. And what is more, these savages have not failed from stupidity; they are, in various degrees of originality, inventive about these matters. You cannot trace the roots of an old perfect system variously maimed and variously dying; you cannot find it, as you find the trace of the Latin language in the mediaeval dialects. On the contrary, you find it beginning—as new scientific discoveries and inventions now begin—here a little and there a little, the same thing half-done in various half-ways, and so as no one who knew the best way would ever have begun. An idea used to prevail that bows and arrows were the "primitive weapons"—the weapons of universal savages; but modern science has made a table,* and some savages

* See the very careful table and admirable discussion in Sir

have them and some have not, and some have substitutes of one sort and some have substitutes of another—several of these substitutes being like the "boomerang," so much more difficult to hit on or to use than the bow, as well as so much less effectual. And not only may the miscellaneous races of the world be justly described as being upon various edges of industrial civilization, approaching it by various sides, and falling short of it in various particulars, but the moment they see the real thing they know how to use it as well as civilized man, or better. The South American uses the horse which the European brought better than the European. Many races use the rifle—the especial and very complicated weapon of civilized man—better, upon an average, than he can use it. The savage with simple tools—tools he appreciates—is like a child, quick to learn, not like an old man, who has once forgotten and who cannot acquire again. Again, if there had been an excellent aboriginal civilization in Australia and America, where, botanists and zoologists ask, are its vestiges? If these savages did care to cultivate wheat, where is the wild wheat gone which their abandoned culture must have left? If they did give up using good domestic animals, what has become of the wild ones which would, according to all natural laws, have sprung up out of them? This much is certain, that the domestic animals of Europe have, since what may be called the

---

John Lubbock's *Pre-Historic Times.* [Lubbock (1834–1913) was an influential naturalist, banker, and statesman. His book *Pre-historic Times,* first published in 1865, was subtitled "As Illustrated by Ancient Remains, and the Manners and Customs of Modern Savages."—*Ed.*]

discovery of the *world* during the last hundred years, run up and down it. The English rat—not the pleasantest of our domestic creatures—has gone everywhere; to Australia, to New Zealand, to America: nothing but a complicated rat-miracle could ever root him out. Nor could a common force expel the horse from South America since the Spaniards took him thither; if we did not know the contrary we should suppose him a principal aboriginal animal. Where then, so to say, are the rats and horses of the primitive civilization? Not only can we not find them, but zoological science tells us that they never existed, for the "feebly pronounced," the ineffectual, marsupials of Australia and New Zealand could never have survived a competition with better creatures, such as that by which they are now perishing.

We catch then a first glimpse of patriarchal man, not with any industrial relics of a primitive civilization, but with some gradually learnt knowledge of the simpler arts, with some tamed animals and some little knowledge of the course of nature as far as it tells upon the seasons and affects the condition of simple tribes. This is what, according to ethnology, we should expect the first historic man to be, and this is what we in fact find him. But what was his mind; how are we to describe that?

I believe the general description in which Sir John Lubbock sums up his estimate of the savage mind suits the patriarchal mind. "Savages," he says, "unite the character of childhood with the passions and strength of men." And if we open the first record of the pagan world —the poems of Homer—how much do we find that suits this description better than any other! Civilization has indeed already gone forward ages beyond the time at which any such description is complete. Man, in Homer, is as good at oratory, Mr. Gladstone* seems to say, as he has ever been, and, much as that means, other and better things might be added to it. But after all, how much of the "splendid savage" there is in Achilles, and how much of the "spoiled child sulking in his tent"! Impressibility and excitability are the main characteristics of the oldest Greek history, and if we turn to the East, the "simple and violent" world, as Mr. Kinglake‡ calls it, of the first times meets us every moment.

And this is precisely what we should expect. An "inherited drill," science says, "makes modern nations what they are; their born structure bears the trace of the laws of their fathers"; but the ancient nations came into no such inheritance; they were the descendants of people who did what was right in their own eyes; they were born to no tutored habits, no preservative bonds, and therefore they were at the mercy of every impulse and blown by every passion.

The condition of the primitive man, if we conceive of him rightly, is, in several respects, different from any we know. We unconsciously assume around us the existence of a great miscellaneous social machine working to our hands, and not only supplying our wants, but even telling and deciding when those wants shall come. No one can now without difficulty conceive how people got on before there were clocks and watches; as Sir George Lewis said, "it takes a vigorous effort of the imagination" to realize a

* [William Ewart Gladstone (1809–1898), English politician and reformer. Prime minister four times: 1868–1874, 1880–1885, 1886, 1892–1894.—*Ed.*]

‡ [Alexander William Kinglake (1809–1891), English travel writer.—*Ed.*]

period when it was a serious difficulty to know the hour of day. And much more is it difficult to fancy the unstable minds of such men as neither knew nature, which is the clock-work of material civilization, nor possessed a polity, which is a kind of clock-work to moral civilization. They never could have known what to expect; the whole habit of steady but varied anticipation, which makes our minds what they are, must have been wholly foreign to theirs.

Again, I at least cannot call up to myself the loose conceptions (as they must have been) of morals which then existed. If we set aside all the element derived from law and polity which runs through our current moral notions, I hardly know what we shall have left. The residuum was somehow, and in some vague way, intelligible to the ante-political man, but it must have been uncertain, wavering, and unfit to be depended upon. In the best cases it existed much as the vague feeling of beauty now exists in minds sensitive but untaught; a still small voice of uncertain meaning; an unknown something modifying everything else, and higher than anything else, yet in form so indistinct that when you looked for it, it was gone or if this be thought the delicate fiction of a later fancy, then morality was at least to be found in the wild spasms of "wild justice," half punishment, half outrage—but anyhow, being unfixed by steady law, it was intermittent, vague, and hard for us to imagine. Everybody who has studied mathematics knows how many shadowy difficulties he seemed to have before he understood the problem, and how impossible it was when once the demonstration had flashed upon him, ever to comprehend those indistinct difficulties again, or to call up the mental confusion that admitted them. So in these days, when we cannot by any effort drive out of our minds the notion of law, we cannot imagine the mind of one who had never known it, and who could not by any effort have conceived it.

Again, the primitive man could not have imagined what we mean by a nation. We on the other hand cannot imagine those to whom it is a difficulty; "we know what it is when you do not ask us," but we cannot very quickly explain or define it. But so much as this is plain, a nation means a *like* body of men, because of that likeness capable of acting together, and because of that likeness inclined to obey similar rules; and even this Homer's Cyclops—used only to sparse human beings—could not have conceived.

To sum up—*law*—rigid, definite, concise law—is the primary want of early mankind; that which they need above anything else, that which is requisite before they can gain anything else. But it is their greatest difficulty, as well as their first requisite; the thing most out of their reach, as well as that most beneficial to them if they reach it. In later ages many races have gained much of this discipline quickly, though painfully; a loose set of scattered clans has been often and often forced to substantial settlement by a rigid conqueror; the Romans did half the work for above half Europe. But where could the first ages find Romans or a conqueror? Men conquer by the power of government, and it was exactly government which then was not. The first ascent of civilization was at a steep gradient, though when now we look down upon it, it seems almost nothing.

III

How the step from polity to no polity was made distinct, history does not record—on this point Sir Henry Maine has drawn a most interesting conclusion from his peculiar studies: "It would be," he tells us,

a very simple explanation of the origin of society if we could base a general conclusion on the hint furnished us by the Scriptural example already adverted to, and could suppose that communities began to exist wherever a family held together instead of separating at the death of its patriarchal chieftain. In most of the Greek states and in Rome there long remained the vestiges of an ascending series of groups out of which the state was at first constituted. The family, house, and tribe of the Romans may be taken as a type of them, and they are so described to us that we can scarcely help conceiving them as a system of concentric circles which have gradually expanded from the same point. The elementary group is the family, connected by common subjection to the highest male ascendant. The aggregation of families forms the *gens*, or house. The aggregation of houses makes the tribe. The aggregation of tribes constitutes the commonwealth. Are we at liberty to follow these indications, and to lay down that the commonwealth is a collection of persons united by common descent from the progenitor of an original family? Of this we may at least be certain, that all ancient societies regarded themselves as having proceeded from one original stock, and even labored under an incapacity for comprehending any reason except this for their holding together in political union. The history of political ideas begins, in fact, with the assumption that kinship in blood is the sole possible ground of community in political functions; nor is there any of those subversions of feeling, which we term emphatically revolu-

tions, so startling and so complete as the change which
is accomplished when some other principle—such as
that, for instance, of *local contiguity*—establishes itself
for the first time as the basis of common political action.*

If this theory were true, the origin of politics would not
seem a great change, or, in early days, be really a great
change. The primacy of the elder brother, in tribes
casually cohesive, would be slight; it would be the beginning of much, but it would be nothing in itself; it would
be—to take an illustration from the opposite end of the
political series—it would be like the headship of a weak
parliamentary leader over adherents who may divide
from him in a moment; it was the germ of sovereignty—it
was hardly yet sovereignty itself.

I do not myself believe that the suggestion of Sir Henry
Maine—for he does not, it will be seen, offer it as a confident theory—is an adequate account of the true origin
of politics. I shall in a subsequent essay show that there
are, as it seems to me, abundant evidences of a time still
older than that which he speaks of. But the theory of Sir
Henry Maine serves my present purpose well. It describes,
and truly describes, a kind of life antecedent to our
present politics, and the conclusion I have drawn from it
will be strengthened, not weakened, when we come to
examine and deal with an age yet older, and a social bond
far more rudimentary.

But when once polities were begun, there is no difficulty in explaining why they lasted. Whatever may be
said against the principle of "natural selection" in other
departments, there is no doubt of its predominance in

* [*Ancient Law*, pages 123–124.—*Ed.*]

early human history. The strongest killed out the weakest, as they could. And I need not pause to prove that any form of polity is more efficient than none; that an aggregate of families owning even a slippery allegiance to a single head would be sure to have the better of a set of families acknowledging no obedience to anyone, but scattering loose about the world and fighting where they stood. Homer's Cyclops would be powerless against the feeblest band; so far from its being singular that we find no other record of that state of man, so unstable and sure to perish was it that we should rather wonder at even a single vestige lasting down to the age when for picturesqueness it became valuable in poetry.

But, though the origin of polity is dubious, we are upon the *terra firma* of actual records when we speak of the preservation of polities. Perhaps every young Englishman who comes nowadays to Aristotle or Plato is struck with their conservatism: fresh from the liberal doctrines of the present age, he wonders at finding in those recognized teachers so much contrary teaching. They both—unlike as they are—hold with Xenophon—so unlike both —that man is the "hardest of all animals to govern." Of Plato it might indeed be plausibly said that the adherents of an intuitive philosophy, being "the Tories of speculation," have commonly been prone to conservatism in government; but Aristotle, the founder of the experience philosophy, ought, according to that doctrine, to have been a liberal, if anyone ever was a liberal. In fact, both of these men lived when men had not "had time to forget" the difficulties of government. We have forgotten them altogether. We reckon, as the basis of our culture, upon an amount of order, of tacit obedience, of prescriptive governability, which these philosophers hoped to get as a principal result of their culture. We take without thought as a *datum* what they hunted as a *quaesitum.**

In early times the quantity of government is much more important than its quality. What you want is a comprehensive rule binding men together, making them do much the same things, telling them what to expect of each other—fashioning them alike, and keeping them so. What this rule is does not matter so much. A good rule is better than a bad one, but any rule is better than none; while, for reasons which a jurist will appreciate, none can be very good. But to gain that rule, what may be called the impressive elements of a polity are incomparably more important than its useful elements. How to get the obedience of men is the hard problem; what you do with that obedience is less critical.

To gain that obedience, the primary condition is the identity—not the union, but the sameness—of what we now call Church and State. Dr. Arnold,‡ fresh from the study of Greek thought and Roman history, used to preach that this identity was the great cure for the misguided modern world. But he spoke to ears filled with other sounds and minds filled with other thoughts, and they hardly knew his meaning, much less heeded it. But though the teaching was wrong for the modern age to which it was applied, it was excellent for the old world from which it was learnt. What is there requisite is a single government—call it Church or State, as you like—regulating the whole of human life. No division of power is then endurable without danger, probably without

---

* [*quaesitum*: a thing sought.—*Ed.*]

‡ [Thomas Arnold (1795–1842), headmaster of Rugby School and father of the poet and critic Matthew Arnold.—*Ed.*]

destruction; the priest must not teach one thing and the king another; king must be priest, and prophet king: the two must say the same, because they are the same. The idea of difference between spiritual penalties and legal penalties must never be awakened. Indeed, early Greek thought or early Roman thought would never have comprehended it. There was a kind of rough public opinion and there were rough, very rough, hands which acted on it. We now talk of political penalties and ecclesiastical prohibition, and the social censure, but they were all one then. Nothing is very like those old communities now, but perhaps a "trade's union" is as near as most things; to work cheap is thought to be a "wicked" thing, and so some Broadhead puts it down.

The object of such organizations is to create what may be called a *cake* of custom. All the actions of life are to be submitted to a single rule for a single object; that gradually created the "hereditary drill" which science teaches to be essential, and which the early instinct of men saw to be essential too. That this *régime* forbids free thought is not an evil; or rather, though an evil, it is the necessary basis for the greatest good; it is necessary for making the mold of civilization, and hardening the soft fiber of early man.

The first recorded history of the Aryan race shows everywhere a king, a council, and, as the necessity of early conflicts required, the king in much prominence and with much power. That there could be in such ages anything like an Oriental despotism, or a Caesarean despotism, was impossible; the outside extra-political army which maintains them could not exist when the tribe was the nation, and when all the men in the tribe were warriors. Hence, in the time of Homer, in the first times of

Rome, in the first times of ancient Germany, the king is the most visible part of the polity, because for momentary welfare he is the most useful. The close oligarchy, the patriciate, which alone could know the fixed law, alone could apply the fixed law, which was recognized as the authorized custodian of the fixed law, had then sole command over the primary social want. It alone knew the code of drill; it alone was obeyed; it alone could drill. Mr. Grote* has admirably described the rise of the primitive oligarchies upon the face of the first monarchy, but perhaps because he so much loves historic Athens, he has not sympathized with prehistoric Athens. He has not shown us the need of a fixed life when all else was unfixed life.

It would be schoolboyish to explain at length how well the two great republics, the two winning republics of the ancient world, embody these conclusions. Rome and Sparta were drilling aristocracies, and succeeded because they were such. Athens was indeed of another and higher order; at least to us instructed moderns who know her and have been taught by her. But to the "Philistines" of those days Athens was of a lower order. She was beaten; she lost the great visible game which is all that short-sighted contemporaries know. She was the great "free failure" of the ancient world. She began, she announced, the good things that were to come; but she was too weak to display and enjoy them; she was trodden down by those of coarser make and better trained frame.

How much these principles are confirmed by Jewish history is obvious. There was doubtless much else in

* [George Grote (1794–1871), Utilitarian reformer and author of the famous multi-volume *History of Greece* (1846–1856). —*Ed.*]

Jewish history—whole elements with which I am not here concerned. But so much is plain. The Jews were in the beginning the most unstable of nations; they were submitted to their law, and they came out the most stable of nations. Their polity was indeed defective in unity. After they asked for a king the spiritual and the secular powers (as we should speak) were never at peace, and never agreed. And the ten tribes who lapsed from their law melted away into the neighboring nations. Jeroboam has been called the "first Liberal"; and, religion apart, there is a meaning in the phrase. He began to break up the binding polity which was what men wanted in that age, though eager and inventive minds always dislike it. But the Jews who adhered to their law became the Jews of the day, a nation of a firm set if ever there was one.

It is connected with this fixity that jurists tell us that the title "contract" is hardly to be discovered in the oldest law. In modern days, in civilized days, men's choice determines nearly all they do. But in early times that choice determined scarcely anything. The guiding rule was the law of *status*. Everybody was born to a place in the community; in that place he had to stay; in that place he found certain duties which he had to fulfill, and which were all he needed to think of. The net of custom caught men in distinct spots, and kept each where he stood.

What are called in European politics the principles of 1789 are therefore inconsistent with the early world; they are fitted only to the new world in which society has gone through its early task; when the inherited organization is already confirmed and fixed; when the soft minds and strong passions of youthful nations are fixed and guided by hard transmitted instincts. Till then not equality before the law is necessary but inequality, for what is most wanted is an elevated *élite* who know the law: not a good government seeking the happiness of its subjects, but a dignified and overawing government getting its subjects to obey: not a good law, but a comprehensive law binding all life to one routine. Later are the ages of freedom; first are the ages of servitude. In 1789, when the great men of the Constituent Assembly looked on the long past, they hardly saw anything in it which could be praised, or admired, or imitated: all seemed a blunder—a complex error to be got rid of as soon as might be. But that error had made themselves. On their very physical organization the hereditary mark of old times was fixed; their brains were hardened and their nerves were steadied by the transmitted results of tedious usages. The ages of monotony had their use, for they trained men for ages when they need not be monotonous.

IV

But even yet we have not realized the full benefit of those early polities and those early laws. They not only "bound up" men in groups, not only impressed on men a certain set of common usages, but often, at least in an indirect way, suggested, if I may use the expression, national character.

We cannot yet explain—I am sure, at least, I can not attempt to explain—all the singular phenomena of national character: how completely and perfectly they seem to be at first framed; how slowly, how gradually they can alone be altered, if they can be altered at all. But there is one analogous fact which may help us to see, at least dimly, how such phenomena are caused. There is a character of *ages*, as well as of nations; and as we have full histories of many such periods, we can examine exactly when and how the mental peculiarity of each began, and also exactly when and how that mental peculiarity passed away. We have an idea of Queen Anne's time, for example, or of Queen Elizabeth's time, or George II's time; or again of the age of Louis XIV, or Louis XV, or the French Revolution; an idea more or less accurate in proportion as we study, but probably even in the minds who know these ages best and most minutely, more special, more simple, more unique than the truth was. We throw aside too much, in making up our images of eras, that which is common to all eras. The English character was much the same in many great respects in Chaucer's time as it was in Elizabeth's time or Anne's time, or as it is now. But some qualities were added to this common element in one era and some in another; some qualities seemed to overshadow and eclipse it in one era, and others in another. We overlook and half forget the constant while we see and watch the variable. But—for that is the present point—*why* is there this variable? Everyone must, I think, have been puzzled about it. Suddenly, in a quiet time—say, in Queen Anne's time—arises a special literature, a marked variety of human expression, pervading what is then written and peculiar to it: surely this is singular.

The true explanation is, I think, something like this. One considerable writer gets a sort of start because what he writes is somewhat more—only a little more very often, as I believe—congenial to the minds around him than any other sort. This writer is very often not the one whom posterity remembers—not the one who carries the style of the age farthest towards its ideal type, and gives it its charm and its perfection. It was not Addison who be-

gan the essay-writing of Queen Anne's time, but Steele;* it
was the vigorous forward man who struck out the rough
notion, though it was the wise and meditative man who
improved upon it and elaborated it, and whom posterity
reads. Some strong writer, or group of writers, thus seize
on the public mind, and a curious process soon assimilates other writers in appearance to them. To some extent,
no doubt, this assimilation is effected by a process most
intelligible, and not at all curious—the process of conscious imitation; A sees that B's style of writing answers,
and he imitates it. But definitely aimed mimicry like this is
always rare; original men who like their own thoughts do
not willingly clothe them in words they feel they borrow.
No man, indeed, can think to much purpose when he is
studying to write a style not his own. After all, very few
men are at all equal to the steady labor, the stupid and
mistaken labor mostly, of *making* a style. Most men catch
the words that are in the air, and the rhythm which comes
to them they do not know from whence; an unconscious
imitation determines their words, and makes them say
what of themselves they would never have thought of
saying. Everyone who has written in more than one
newspaper knows how invariably his style catches the
tone of each paper while he is writing for it, and changes
to the tone of another when in turn he begins to write for
that. He probably would rather write the traditional style
to which the readers of the journal are used, but he does
not set himself to copy it; he would have to force himself

---

* [Joseph Addison (1672–1719), classical scholar and influential essayist. He collaborated with the journalist Sir Richard
Steele (1672–1729) on *The Tatler* and the original *Spectator*
magazine.—*Ed.*]

in order *not* to write it if that was what he wanted. Exactly in this way, just as a writer for a journal without a distinctly framed purpose gives the readers of the journal the sort of words and the sort of thoughts they are used to—so, on a larger scale, the writers of an age, without thinking of it, give to the readers of the age the sort of words and the sort of thoughts—the special literature, in fact—which those readers like and prize. And not only does the writer, without thinking, choose the sort of style and meaning which are most in vogue, but the writer is himself chosen. A writer does not begin to write in the traditional rhythm of an age unless he feels, or fancies he feels, a sort of aptitude for writing it, any more than a writer tries to write in a journal in which the style is uncongenial or impossible to him. Indeed, if he mistakes he is soon weeded out; the editor rejects, the age will not read his compositions. How painfully this traditional style cramps great writers whom it happens not to suit is curiously seen in Wordsworth, who was bold enough to break through it, and, at the risk of contemporary neglect, to frame a style of his own. But he did so knowingly, and he did so with an effort. "It is supposed," he says,

that by the act of writing in verse an author makes a formal engagement that he will gratify certain known habits of association; that he not only then apprises the reader that certain classes of ideas and expressions will be found in his book, but that others will be carefully eschewed. The exponent or symbol held forth by metrical language must, in different ages of literature, have excited very different expectations; for example, in the age of Catullus, Terence, or Lucretius, and that of Statius or Claudian; and in our own country, in the age of Shakespeare and Beaumont and Fletcher, and that of Donne and Cowley or Dryden or Pope.*

And then, in a kind of vexed way, Wordsworth goes on to explain that he himself can't and won't do what is expected from him, but that he will write his own words, and only his own words. A strict, I was going to say a Puritan, genius will act thus, but most men of genius are susceptible and versatile, and fall into the style of their age. One very unapt at the assimilating process, but on that account the more curious about it, says:

> How we
> Track a live long day, great heaven, and watch
> our shadows!
> What our shadows seem, forsooth, we will ourselves be.
> Do I look like that? You think me that: then I *am* that.

What writers are expected to write, they write; or else they do not write at all; but, like the writer of these lines, stop discouraged, live disheartened, and die leaving fragments which their friends treasure, but which a rushing world never heeds. The nonconformist writers are neglected, the conformist writers are encouraged, until perhaps on a sudden the fashion shifts. And as with the writers, so in a less degree with readers. Many men—most men—get to like or think they like that which is ever before them, and which those around them like, and which received opinion says they ought to like; or if their minds are too marked and oddly made to get into the

* [From the beginning of Wordsworth's *Preface* to the second edition of *Lyrical Ballads* (1800).—*Ed.*]

mold, they give up reading altogether, or read old books and foreign books, formed under another code and appealing to a different taste. The principle of "elimination," the "use and disuse" of organs which naturalists speak of, works here. What is used strengthens; what is disused weakens: "to those who have, more is given"; and so a sort of style settles upon an age, and imprinting itself more than anything else in men's memories becomes all that is thought of about it.

I believe that what we call national character arose in very much the same way. At first a sort of "chance predominance" made a model, and then invincible attraction, the necessity which rules all but the strongest men to imitate what is before their eyes, and to be what they are expected to be, molded men by that model. This is, I think, the very process by which new national characters are being made in our own time. In America and in Australia a new modification of what we call Anglo-Saxonism is growing. A sort of type of character arose from the difficulties of colonial life—the difficulty of struggling with the wilderness; and this type has given its shape to the mass of characters because the mass of characters have unconsciously imitated it. Many of the American characteristics are plainly useful in such a life, and consequent on such a life. The eager restlessness, the highly-strung nervous organization are useful in continual struggle, and also are promoted by it. These traits seem to be arising in Australia, too, and wherever else the English race is placed in like circumstances. But even in these useful particulars the innate tendency of the human mind to become like what is around it has effected much; a sluggish Englishman will often catch the eager American look in a few years; an Irishman or even a German will catch it, too, even in all English particulars. And as to a hundred minor points—in so many that go to mark the typical Yankee—usefulness has had no share either in their origin or their propagation. The accident of some predominant person possessing them set the fashion, and it has been imitated to this day. Anybody who inquires will find even in England, and even in these days of assimilation, parish peculiarities which arose, no doubt, from some old accident and have been heedfully preserved by customary copying. A national character is but the successful parish character; just as the national speech is but the successful parish dialect, the dialect, that is, of the district which came to be more—in many cases but a little more—influential than other districts, and so set its yoke on books and on society.

I could enlarge much on this, for I believe this unconscious imitation to be the principal force in the making of national characters; but I have already said more about it than I need. Everybody who weighs even half these arguments will admit that it is a great force in the matter, a principal agency to be acknowledged and watched; and for my present purpose I want no more. I have only to show the efficacy of the tight early polity (so to speak) and the strict early law on the creation of corporate characters. These settled the predominant type, set up a sort of model, made a sort of *idol*; this was worshipped, copied, and observed, from all manner of mingled feelings, but most of all because it was the "thing to do," the then accepted form of human action. When once the predominant type was determined, the copying propensity of man did the rest. The tradition ascribing Spartan legislation to Lycurgus was literally untrue, but its spirit was quite true. In the origin of states strong and eager individuals got hold of small knots of men and made for them a fashion which they were attached to and kept.

It is only after duly apprehending the silent manner in which national characters thus form themselves that we can rightly appreciate the dislike which old governments had to trade. There must have been something peculiar about it, for the best philosophers, Plato and Aristotle, shared it. They regarded commerce as the source of corruption as naturally as a modern economist considers it the spring of industry, and all the old governments acted in this respect upon the philosophers' maxims. "Well," said Dr. Arnold, speaking ironically and in the spirit of modern times—"Well, indeed, might the policy of the old priest-nobles of Egypt and India endeavor to divert their people from becoming familiar with the sea, and represent the occupation of a seaman as incompatible with the purity of the highest castes. The sea deserved to be hated by the old aristocracies, inasmuch as it has been the mightiest instrument in the civilization of mankind." But the old oligarchies had their own work, as we now know. They were imposing a fashioning yoke; they were making the human nature which after times employ. They were at their labors, we have entered into these labors. And to the unconscious imitation which was their principal tool, no impediment was so formidable as foreign intercourse. Men imitate what is before their eyes, if it is before their eyes alone, but they do not imitate it if it is only one among many present things—one competitor among others, all of which are equal and some of which seem better. "Whoever speaks two languages is a rascal," says the saying, and it rightly represents the feeling of primitive communities when the sudden impact of new thoughts and new examples breaks down the compact despotism of the single consecrated code, and leaves pliant and impressible man—such as he then is—to follow his unpleasant will without distinct guidance by hereditary morality and hereditary religion. The old oligarchies wanted to keep their type perfect, and for that end they were right not to allow foreigners to touch it.

"Distinctions of race," says Arnold himself elsewhere in a remarkable essay*—for it was his last on Greek history, his farewell words on a long favorite subject—"were not of that odious and fantastic character which they have borne in modern times; they implied real differences of the most important kind, religious and moral." And after exemplifying this at length he goes on:

> It is not then to be wondered at that Thucydides, when speaking of a city founded jointly by Ionians and Dorians, should have thought it right to add that "the prevailing institutions of the place were the Ionian," for according as they were derived from one or the other of the two places the whole character of the people would be different. And therefore the mixture of persons of different race in the same commonwealth, unless one race had a complete ascendancy, tended to confuse all the relations of life, and all men's notions of right and wrong; or by compelling men to tolerate in so near a relation as that of fellow-citizens differences upon the main points of human life, led to a general carelessness and scepticism, and encouraged

* [This quotation is from Arnold's preface to the third volume of his edition of Thucydides' *History of the Peloponnesian War* (Oxford: John Henry Parker, 1842), page xvii.—*Ed.*]

the notion that right and wrong had no real existence,
but are mere creatures of human opinion.

But if this be so, the oligarchies were right. Commerce
brings this mingling of ideas, this breaking down of old
creeds, and brings it inevitably. It is nowadays its greatest
good that it does so; the change is what we call "enlargement of mind." But in early times Providence "set apart
the nations"; and it is not till the frame of their morals is
set by long ages of transmitted discipline that such enlargement can be borne. The ages of isolation had their
use, for they trained men for ages when they were not to
be isolated.

2

The Use of Conflict

I

"T HE DIFFERENCE between progression and stationary
inaction," says one of our greatest living writers, "is
one of the great secrets which science has yet to penetrate." I am sure I do not pretend that I can completely
penetrate it; but it undoubtedly seems to me that the
problem is on the verge of solution, and that scientific
successes in kindred fields by analogy suggest some principles which wholly remove many of its difficulties, and
indicate the sort of way in which those which remain may
hereafter be removed too.

But what is the problem? Common English, I might
perhaps say common civilized thought, ignores it. Our
habitual instructors, our ordinary conversation, our inevitable and ineradicable prejudices tend to make us think
that "progress" is the normal fact in human society, the
fact which we should expect to see, the fact which we
should be surprised if we did not see. But history refutes
this. The ancients had no conception of progress; they did
not so much as reject the idea; they did not even entertain
the idea. Oriental nations are just the same now. Since
history began they have always been what they are. Sav-

ages, again, do not improve; they hardly seem to have the basis on which to build, much less the material to put up anything worth having. Only a few nations, and those of European origin, advance; and yet these think—seem irresistibly compelled to think—such advance to be inevitable, natural, and eternal. Why then is this great contrast?

Before we can answer, we must investigate more accurately. No doubt history shows that most nations are stationary now; but it affords reason to think that all nations once advanced. Their progress was arrested at various points; but nowhere, probably not even in the hill tribes of India, not even in the Andaman Islanders, not even in the savages of Tierra del Fuego, do we find men who have not got some way. They have made their little progress in a hundred different ways; they have framed with infinite assiduity a hundred curious habits; they have, so to say, *screwed* themselves into the uncomfortable corners of a complex life, which is odd and dreary, but yet is possible. And the corners are never the same in any two parts of the world. Our record begins with a thousand unchanging edifices, but it shows traces of previous building. In historic times there has been little progress; in prehistoric times there must have been much.

In solving, or trying to solve, the question, we must take notice of this remarkable difference, and explain it, too, or else we may be sure our principles are utterly incomplete, and perhaps altogether unsound. But what then is that solution, or what are the principles which tend towards it? Three laws, or approximate laws, may, I think, be laid down, with only one of which I can deal in this paper, but all three of which it will be best to state, that it may be seen what I am aiming at.

First. In every particular state of the world, those nations which are strongest tend to prevail over the others; and in certain marked peculiarities the strongest tend to be the best.

Secondly. Within every particular nation the type or types of character then and there most attractive tend to prevail; and the most attractive, though with exceptions, is what we call the best character.

Thirdly. Neither of these competitions is in most historic conditions intensified by extrinsic forces, but in some conditions, such as those now prevailing in the most influential part of the world, both are so intensified.

These are the sort of doctrines with which, under the name of "natural selection" in physical science, we have become familiar; and as every great scientific conception tends to advance its boundaries and to be of use in solving problems not thought of when it was started, so here, what was put forward for mere animal history may, with a change of form, but an identical essence, be applied to human history.

At first some objection was raised to the principle of "natural selection" in physical science upon religious grounds; it was to be expected that so active an idea and so large a shifting of thought would seem to imperil much which men valued. But in this, as in other cases, the objection is, I think, passing away; the new principle is more and more seen to be fatal to mere outworks of religion, not to religion itself. At all events, to the sort of application here made of it, which only amounts to searching out and following up an analogy suggested by it, there is plainly no objection. Everyone now admits that human history is guided by certain laws, and all that is here aimed at is to indicate, in a more or less distinct way, an infinitesimally small portion of such laws.

The discussion of these three principles cannot be kept quite apart except by pedantry; but it is almost exclusively with the first—that of the competition between nation and nation, or tribe and tribe (for I must use these words in their largest sense, and so as to include every cohering aggregate of human beings)—that I can deal now; and even as to that I can but set down a few principal considerations.

The progress of the military art is the most conspicuous, I was about to say the most *showy*, fact in human history. Ancient civilization may be compared with modern in many respects, and plausible arguments constructed to show that it is better; but you cannot compare the two in military power. Napoleon could indisputably have conquered Alexander; our Indian army would not think much of the Retreat of the Ten Thousand. And I suppose the improvement has been continuous: I have not the slightest pretense to special knowledge; but, looking at the mere surface of the facts, it seems likely that the aggregate battle array, so to say, of mankind, the fighting force of the human race, has constantly and invariably grown. It is true that the ancient civilization long resisted the "barbarians," and was then destroyed by the barbarians. But the barbarians had improved. "By degrees," says a most accomplished writer,* "barbarian mercenaries came to form the largest, or at least the most effective, part of the Roman armies. The

---

* Mr. Bryce. [James Bryce (1832–1922), 1st Viscount, diplomat, historian, and Regius professor of civil law at Oxford. This quotation is from *The Holy Roman Empire*, Chapter 3, "The Barbarian Invasions" (Fourth Edition, London: Macmillan, 1932), pages 15–16.—*Ed.*]

bodyguard of Augustus had been so composed; the prae-torians were generally selected from the bravest frontier troops, most of them Germans." "Thus," he continues, "in many ways was the old antagonism broken down, Romans admitting barbarians to rank and office; bar-barians catching something of the manners and culture of their neighbours. And thus, when the final movement came, the Teutonic tribes slowly established themselves through the provinces, knowing something of the system to which they came, and not unwilling to be considered its members." Taking friend and foe together, it may be doubted whether the fighting capacity of the two armies was not as great at last, when the empire fell, as ever it was in the long period while the empire prevailed. During the Middle Ages the combining power of men often failed; in a divided time you cannot collect as many sol-diers as in a concentrated time. But this difficulty is political, not military. If you added up the many little hosts of any century of separation, they would perhaps be found equal to or greater than the single host, or the fewer hosts, of previous centuries which were more united. Taken as a whole, and allowing for possible ex-ceptions, the aggregate fighting power of mankind has grown immensely, and has been growing continuously since we knew anything about it.

Again, this force has tended to concentrate itself more and more in certain groups which we call "civilized na-tions." The *literati* of the last century were for ever in fear of a new conquest of the barbarians, but only because their imagination was overshadowed and frightened by the old conquests. A very little consideration would have shown them that, since the monopoly of military inven-tions by cultivated states, real and effective military power tends to confine itself to those states. The barbarians are no longer so much as vanquished competitors; they have ceased to compete at all.

The military vices, too, of civilization seem to decline just as its military strength augments. Somehow or other civilization does not make men effeminate or unwarlike now as it once did. There is an improvement in our fiber —moral, if not physical. In ancient times city people could not be got to fight—seemingly could not fight; they lost their mental courage, perhaps their bodily nerve. But nowadays in all countries the great cities could pour out multitudes wanting nothing but practice to make good soldiers, and abounding in bravery and vigor. This was so in America; it was so in Prussia; and it would be so in England too. The breed of ancient times was impaired for war by trade and luxury, but the modern breed is not so impaired.

A curious fact indicates the same thing probably, if not certainly. Savages waste away before modern civilization; they seem to have held their ground before the ancient. There is no lament in any classical writer for the barbarians. The New Zealanders say that the land will depart from their children; the Australians are vanishing; the Tasmanians have vanished. If anything like this had happened in antiquity, the classical moralists would have been sure to muse over it; for it is just the large solemn kind of fact that suited them. On the contrary, in Gaul, in Spain, in Sicily—everywhere that we know of—the barbarian endured the contact of the Roman, and the Roman allied himself to the barbarian. Modern science explains the wasting away of savage men; it says that we have diseases which we can bear, though they cannot, and that they die away before them as our fatted and protected cattle died out before the rinderpest, which is innocuous, in comparison, to the hardy cattle of the steppes. Savages in the first year of the Christian era were pretty much what they were in the 1800th; and if they stood the contact of ancient civilized men, and cannot stand ours, it follows that our race is presumably tougher than the ancient; for we have to bear, and do bear, the seeds of greater diseases than those the ancients carried with them. We may use, perhaps, the unvarying savage as a meter to gauge the vigor of the constitutions to whose contact he is exposed.

Particular consequences may be dubious, but as to the main fact there is no doubt: the military strength of man has been growing from the earliest time known to our history, straight on till now. And we must not look at times known by written records only; we must travel back to older ages, known to us only by what lawyers call *real* evidence—the evidence of things. Before history began, there was at least as much progress in the military art as there has been since. The Roman legionaries or Homeric Greeks were about as superior to the men of the shell mounds and the flint implements as we are superior to them. There has been a constant acquisition of military strength by man since we know anything of him, either by the documents he has composed or the indications he has left.

The cause of this military growth is very plain. The strongest nation has always been conquering the weaker; sometimes even subduing it, but always prevailing over it. Every intellectual gain, so to speak, that a nation possessed was in the earliest times made use of—was *invested* and taken out—in war; all else perished. Each nation tried constantly to be the stronger, and so made or copied the best weapons; by conscious and unconscious imitation each nation formed a type of character suitable to war and conquest. Conquest improved mankind by the intermixture of strengths; the armed truce, which was then called peace, improved them by the competition of training and the consequent creation of new power. Since the long-headed men first drove the short-headed men out of the best land in Europe, all European history has been the history of the superposition of the more military races over the less military—of the efforts, sometimes successful, sometimes unsuccessful, of each race to get more military; and so the art of war has constantly improved.

But why is one nation stronger than another? In the answer to that, I believe, lies the key to the principal progress of early civilization, and to some of the progress of all civilization. The answer is that there are very many advantages—some small and some great—every one of which tends to make the nation which has it superior to the nation which has it not; that many of these advantages can be imparted to subjugated races, or imitated by competing races; and that, though some of these advantages may be perishable or inimitable, yet, on the whole, the energy of civilization grows by the coalescence of strengths and by the competition of strengths.

II

By far the greatest advantage is that on which I observed before—that to which I drew all the attention I was able by making the first of these essays an essay on the Preliminary Age. The first thing to acquire is, if I may so express it, the *legal fiber*; a polity first—what sort of polity is immaterial; a law first—what kind of law is secondary; a person or set of persons to pay deference to—though who he is, or they are, by comparison scarcely signifies.

"There is," it has been said, "hardly any exaggerating the difference between civilized and uncivilized men; it is greater than the difference between a tame and a wild animal," because man can improve more. But the difference at first was gained in much the same way. The taming of animals as it now goes on among savage nations, and as travelers who have seen it describe it, is a kind of selection. The most wild are killed when food is wanted, and the most tame and easy to manage kept, because they are more agreeable to human indolence, and so the keeper likes them best. Captain Galton, who has often seen strange scenes of savage and of animal life, had better describe the process: "The irreclaimably wild members of every flock would escape and be utterly lost; the wilder of those that remained would assuredly be selected for slaughter whenever it was necessary that one of the flock should be killed. The tamest cattle—those which seldom ran away, that kept the flocks together, and those which led them homeward—would be preserved alive longer than any of the others. It is, therefore, these that chiefly become the parents of stock and bequeath their domestic aptitudes to the future herd. I have constantly witnessed this process of selection among the pastoral savages of South Africa. I believe it to be a very important one on account of its rigor and its regularity. It must have existed from the earliest times, and have been in continuous operation, generation after generation, down to the present day."*

* Ethnological Society's *Transactions*, Vol. III, page 137. [Sir

Man, being the strongest of all animals, differs from the rest; he was obliged to be his own domesticator; he had to tame himself. And the way in which it happened was that the most obedient, the tamest tribes are, at the first stage in the real struggle of life, the strongest and the conquerors. All are very wild then; the animal vigor, the savage virtue of the race has died out in none, and all have enough of it. But what makes one tribe one incipient tribe, one bit of a tribe—to differ from another is their relative faculty of coherence. The slightest symptom of legal development, the least indication of a military bond, is then enough to turn the scale. The compact tribes win, and the compact tribes are the tamest. Civilization begins, because the beginning of civilization is a military advantage.

Probably if we had historic records of the ante-historic ages—if some superhuman power had set down the thoughts and actions of men ages before they could set them down for themselves—we should know that this first step in civilization was the hardest step. But when we come to history as it is, we are more struck with the difficulty of the next step. All the absolutely incoherent men—all the "Cyclopes"—have been cleared away long before there was an authentic account of them. And the least coherent only remain in the "protected" parts of the world, as we may call them. Ordinary civilization begins

***

Francis Galton (1822–1911), British scientist, cousin of Charles Darwin, and founder of eugenics, a term he coined. This passage is from "The First Steps Towards the Domestication of Animals," *Transactions of the Ethnological Society of London* (London: John Murray, 1865).—Ed.]

near the Mediterranean Sea; the best, doubtless, of the ante-historic civilizations were not far off. From this center the conquering *swarm*—for such it is has grown and grown; has widened its subject territories steadily, though not equably, age by age. But geography long defied it. An Atlantic Ocean, a Pacific Ocean, an Australian Ocean, an unapproachable interior Africa, an inaccessible and undesirable hill India, were beyond its range. In such remote places there was no real competition, and on them inferior half-combined men continued to exist. But in the regions of rivalry—the regions where the better man pressed upon the worse man—such half-made associations could not last. They died out, and history did not begin till after they were gone. The great difficulty which history records is not that of the first step, but that of the second step. What is most evident is not the difficulty of getting a fixed law, but getting out of a fixed law; not of cementing (as upon a former occasion I phrased it) a cake of custom, but of breaking the cake of custom; not of making the first preservative habit, but of breaking through it, and reaching something better.

This is the precise case with the whole family of arrested civilizations. A large part, a very large part, of the world seems to be ready to advance to something good— to have prepared all the means to advance to something good—and then to have stopped and not advanced. India, Japan, China, almost every sort of Oriental civilization, though differing in nearly all other things, are in this alike. They look as if they had paused when there was no reason for pausing—when a mere observer from without would say they were likely not to pause.

The reason is that only those nations can progress which preserve and use the fundamental peculiarity which

was given by nature to man's organism as to all other or-
ganisms. By a law of which we know no reason, but
which is among the first by which Providence guides and
governs the world, there is a tendency in descendants to
be like their progenitors, and yet a tendency also in descendants to *differ* from their progenitors. The work of
nature in making generations is a patchwork—part resemblance, part contrast. In certain respects each born
generation is not like the last born; and in certain other
respects it is like the last. But the peculiarity of arrested
civilization is to kill out varieties at birth almost; that is,
in early childhood, and before they can develop. The
fixed custom which public opinion alone tolerates is imposed on all minds, whether it suits them or not. In that
case the community feel that this custom is the only shel-
ter from bare tyranny, and the only security for what they
value. Most Oriental communities live on land which in
theory is the property of a despotic sovereign, and neither
they nor their families could have the elements of decent
existence unless they held the land upon some sort of
fixed terms. Land in that state of society is (for all but a
petty skilled minority) a necessary of life, and all the un-
increasable land being occupied, a man who is turned out
of his holding is turned out of this world, and must die.
And our notion of written leases is as out of place in a
world without writing and without reading as a House of
Commons among Andaman Islanders. Only one check,
one sole shield for life and good, is then possible—usage.
And it is but too plain how in such places and periods
men cling to customs because customs alone stand between them and starvation.

A still more powerful cause co-operated, if a cause

more powerful can be imagined. Dryden* had a dream of an early age "when wild in woods the noble savage ran"; but "when lone in woods the cringing savage crept" would have been more like all we know of that early, bare, painful period. Not only had they no comfort, no convenience, not the very beginnings of an epicurean life, but their mind within was as painful to them as the world without. It was full of fear. So far as the vestiges inform us, they were afraid of everything; they were afraid of animals, of certain attacks by near tribes, and of possible inroads from far tribes. But, above all things, they were frightened of "the world"; the spectacle of nature filled them with awe and dread. They fancied there were powers behind it which must be pleased, soothed, flattered, and this very often in a number of hideous ways. We have too many such religions, even among races of great cultivation. Men change their religions more slowly than they change anything else; and accordingly we have religions "of the ages" (it is Mr. Jowett‡ who so calls them)—of the "ages before morality"; of ages of which the civil life, the common maxims, and all the secular thoughts have long been dead. "Every reader of the classics," said Dr. Johnson, "finds their mythology tedious." In that old world, which is so like our modern world in so many things, so much more like than many far more

* [John Dryden (1631–1700), English poet.—*Ed.*]

‡ [Benjamin Jowett (1817–1893), professor of Greek and master of Balliol College, Oxford, was an immensely influential teacher. Although they were much criticized by scholars, his translations of classical texts—especially of Plato's *Dialogues*—gained a wide popular following.—*Ed.*]

recent, or some that live beside us, there is a part in which we seem to have no kindred, which we stare at, of which we cannot think how it could be credible, or how it came to be thought of. This is the archaic part of that very world which we look at as so ancient; an "antiquity" which descended to them, hardly altered, perhaps, from times long antecedent, which were as unintelligible to them as to us, or more so. How this terrible religion—for such it was in all living detail, though we make, and the ancients then made, an artistic use of the more attractive bits of it—weighed on man, the great poem of Lucretius, the most of a nineteenth-century poem of any in antiquity, brings before us with a feeling so vivid as to be almost a feeling of our own. Yet the classical religion is a mild and tender specimen of the preserved religions. To get at the worst, you should look where the destroying competition has been least—at America, where sectional civilization was rare, and a pervading coercive civilization did not exist; at such religions as those of the Aztecs.

At first sight it seems impossible to imagine what conceivable function such awful religions can perform in the economy of the world. And no one can fully explain them. But one use they assuredly had: they fixed the yoke of custom thoroughly on mankind. They were the prime agents of the era. They put upon a fixed law a sanction so fearful that no one could dream of not conforming to it.

No one will ever comprehend the arrested civilizations unless he sees the strict dilemma of early society. Either men had no law at all, and lived in confused tribes, hardly hanging together, or they had to obtain a fixed law by processes of incredible difficulty. Those who surmounted that difficulty soon destroyed all those that lay in their way who did not. And then they themselves were caught in their own yoke. The customary discipline, which could only be imposed on any early men by terrible sanctions, continued with those sanctions, and killed out of the whole society the propensities to variation which are the principle of progress.

Experience shows how incredibly difficult it is to get men really to encourage the principle of originality. They will admit it in theory, but in practice the old error—the error which arrested a hundred civilizations—returns again. Men are too fond of their own life, too credulous of the completeness of their own ideas, too angry at the pain of new thoughts, to be able to bear easily with a changing existence; or else, *having* new ideas, they want to enforce them on mankind—to make them heard, and admitted, and obeyed before, in simple competition with other ideas, they would ever be so naturally. At this very moment there are the most rigid Comtists teaching that we ought to be governed by a hierarchy—a combination of savants orthodox in science. Yet who can doubt that Comte would have been hanged by his own hierarchy; that his *essor matériel*, which was in fact troubled by the "theologians and metaphysicians" of the Polytechnic School, would have been more impeded by the government he wanted to make? And then the secular Comtists, Mr. Harrison and Mr. Beesly,* who want to "Frenchify the English institutions"—that is, to introduce—here an imitation of the Napoleonic system, a dictatorship

---

* [Auguste Comte (1798–1857), French social philosopher and founder of Positivism, was an enormous influence on English Utilitarianism. Frederic Harrison (1831–1923) and Edward Spencer Beesly (1831–1915) were British writers and activist disciples of Comte.—*Ed.*]

founded on the proletariat—who can doubt that if both these clever writers had been real Frenchmen they would have been irascible anti-Bonapartists, and have been sent to Cayenne long ere now? The wish of these writers is very natural. They want to "organize society," to erect a despot who will do what they like and work out their ideas; but any despot will do what he himself likes, and will root out new ideas ninety-nine times for once that he introduces them.

Again, side by side with these Comtists, and warring with them—at least with one of them—is Mr. Arnold,* whose poems we know by heart, and who has, as much as any living Englishman, the genuine literary impulse; and yet even he wants to put a yoke upon us—and, worse than a political yoke, an academic yoke, a yoke upon our minds and our styles. He, too, asks us to imitate France; and what else can we say than what the two most thorough Frenchmen of the last age did say?—"Dans les corps à talent, nulle distinction ne fait ombrage, si ce n'est celle du talent. Un duc et pair honore l'Académie Française, qui ne veut point de Boileau, refuse la Bruyère, fait attendre Voltaire, mais reçoit tout d'abord Chapelain et Conrart. De même nous voyons à l'Académie grecque le vicomte invité, Coraï repoussé, lorsque Jomard y entre comme dans un moulin." Thus speaks Paul-Louis Courier‡

---

* [The critic and poet Matthew Arnold (1822–1888), eldest son of Thomas Arnold. Bagehot probably has in mind Arnold's famous essay "The Literary Influence of Academies," which extols the literary and intellectual authority represented by the French Academy.—*Ed.*]

‡ [Paul-Louis Courier (1772–1825), pamphleteer and scholar. "In groups of Talented People [such as in the Academies],

in his own brief inimitable prose. And a still greater writer—a real Frenchman, if ever there was one, and (what many critics would have denied to be possible) a great poet by reason of his *most* French characteristics—Béranger, tells us in verse:

Je croyais voir le président
Faire bâiller—en répondant
Que l'on vient de perdre un grand homme;
Que moi je le vaux, Dieu sait comme.
Mais ce président sans façon*
Ne pérore ici qu'en chanson:
Toujours trop tôt sa harangue est finie.
Non, non, ce n'est point comme à l'Académie.
Ce n'est point comme à l'Académie.

---

the only distinction that doesn't cast a shadow is talent. The Academie Française honors a duke and peer, but doesn't want Boileau at all, refuses la Bruyère, makes Voltaire wait, yet immediately admits [the insignificant writers] Chapelain and Conrart. At the same time, we see at the Greek academy a Viscount is accepted, Coraï is turned away, while Jomard enters as if anybody can walk in." This passage is from "Lettre à MM. de l'Académie," which appears in *Lettres écrites de France et d'Italie. Oeuvres Complètes* (Paris: Gallimard, 1951), page 277.—*Ed.*]

* Désaugiers. [The verses Bagehot quotes are from "L'Académie et le Caveau" by Pierre-Jean de Béranger (1780–1857), French poet and author of *Chansons*, popular collections of satirical light verse. See *Oeuvres complètes, tome premier* (Paris: Editions d'aujourd'hui, 1983), pages 9–10. The poem contrasts the stuffiness of the Académie Française

Admis enfin, aurai-je alors,
Pour tout esprit, l'esprit de corps?
Il rend le bon sens, quoi qu'on dise,
Solidaire de la sottise;
Mais, dans votre société,
L'esprit de corps, c'est la gaîté;
Cet esprit-là régne sans tyrannie.
Non, non, ce n'est point comme à l'Académie;
Ce n'est point comme à l'Académie.

Asylums of commonplace, he hints, academies must ever be. But that sentence is too harsh; the true one is— the academies are asylums of the ideas and the tastes of the last age. "By the time," I have heard a most eminent man of science observe, "by the time a man of science

---

with the convivial alternative, called Le Caveau moderne, whose members included Marc-Antoine Désaugiers, a writer of songs and light verse whom Bagehot identifies above, and Brillat-Savarin, the celebrated author of *La Physiologie du Goût* (1825).

"I thought I'd see the president yawn while answering that we just lost a great man, that I was worthy of joining— the Lord knows how! But here, this president has no ceremony but a song—his speech is always over too soon. No, no, this is not at all like the Academy, nothing like the Academy.

"Finally admitted, would my spirit be taken over by group-think? No matter what anyone says, it makes a lot of sense: solidarity in foolishness. But in your society, light-heartedness is the reigning spirit—it reigns without tyranny. No, no, this is not at all like the Academy, nothing like the Academy."—*Ed.*]

attains eminence on any subject, he becomes a nuisance upon it, because he is sure to retain errors which were in vogue when he was young, but which the new race have refuted." These are the sort of ideas which find their home in academies, and out of their dignified windows pooh-pooh new things.

I may seem to have wandered far from early society, but I have not wandered. The true scientific method is to explain the past by the present—what we see by what we do not see. We can only comprehend why so many nations have not varied, when we see how hateful variation is; how everybody turns against it; how not only the conservatives of speculation try to root it out, but the very innovators invent most rigid machines for crushing the "monstrosities and anomalies"—the new forms, out of which, by competition and trial, the best is to be selected for the future. The point I am bringing out is simple: one most important prerequisite of a prevailing nation is that it should have passed out of the first stage of civilization into the second stage, out of the stage where permanence is most wanted into that where variability is most wanted; and you cannot comprehend why progress is so slow till you see how hard the most obstinate tendencies of human nature make that step to mankind.

Of course the nation we are supposing must keep the virtues of its first stage as it passes into the after stage, else it will be trodden out; it will have lost the savage virtues in getting the beginning of the civilized virtues; and the savage virtues which tend to war are the daily bread of human nature. Carlyle* said, in his graphic way:

* [Thomas Carlyle (1795–1881), Scottish critic, historian, and polemicist.—*Ed.*]

"The ultimate question between every two human beings is, 'Can I kill thee, or canst thou kill me?'" History is strewn with the wrecks of nations which have gained a little progressiveness at the cost of a great deal of hard manliness, and have thus prepared themselves for destruction as soon as the movements of the world gave a chance for it. But these nations have come out of the "pre-economic stage" too soon; they have been put to learn while yet only too apt to unlearn. Such cases do not vitiate, they confirm, the principle—that a nation which has just gained variability without losing legality has a singular likelihood to be a prevalent nation.

No nation admits of an abstract definition; all nations are beings of many qualities and many sides; no historical event exactly illustrates any one principle; every cause is intertwined and surrounded with a hundred others. The best history is but like the art of Rembrandt; it casts a vivid light on certain selected causes, on those which were best and greatest; it leaves all the rest in shadow and unseen. To make a single nation illustrate a principle, you must exaggerate much and you must omit much. But, not forgetting this caution, did not Rome—the prevalent nation in the ancient world—gain her predominance by the principle on which I have dwelt? In the thick crust of her legality there was hidden a little seed of adaptiveness. Even in her law itself no one can fail to see that, binding as was the habit of obedience, coercive as use and wont at first seem, a hidden impulse of extrication *did* manage, in some queer way, to change the substance while conforming to the accidents—to do what was wanted for the new time while seeming to do only what was directed by the old time. And the moral of their whole history is the same: each Roman generation, so far as we know, differs a little—and in the best times often but a *very* little from its predecessors. And therefore the history is so continuous as it goes, though its two ends are so unlike. The history of many nations is like the stage of the English drama: one scene is succeeded on a sudden by a scene quite different—a cottage by a palace, and a windmill by a fortress. But the history of Rome changes as a good diorama changes; while you look, you hardly see it alter; each moment is hardly different from the last moment; yet at the close the metamorphosis is complete, and scarcely anything is as it began. Just so in the history of the great prevailing city: you begin with a town and you end with an empire, and this by unmarked stages. So shrouded, so shielded, in the coarse fiber of other qualities was the delicate principle of progress that it never failed, and it was never broken.

One standing instance, no doubt, shows that the union of progressiveness and legality does not secure supremacy in war. The Jewish nation has its type of progress in the prophets, side by side with its type of permanence in the law and Levites, more distinct than any other ancient people. Nowhere in common history do we see the two forces—both so necessary and both so dangerous—so apart and so intense: Judaea changed in inward thought, just as Rome changed in exterior power. Each change was continuous, gradual, and good. In early times every sort of advantage tends to become a military advantage; such is the best way, then, to keep it alive. But the Jewish advantage never did so; beginning in religion, contrary to a thousand analogies, it remained religious. *For* that we care for them; *from* that have issued endless consequences. But I cannot deal with such matters here, nor are they to my purpose. As respects this essay, Judaea is an example of combined variability and legality not investing itself in warlike power, and so perishing at last, but bequeathing nevertheless a legacy of the combination in imperishable mental effects.

It may be objected that this principle is like saying that men walk when they do walk, and sit when they do sit. The problem is, why do men progress? And the answer suggested seems to be that they progress when they have a certain sufficient amount of variability in their nature. This seems to be the old style of explanation by occult qualities. It seems like saying that opium sends men to sleep because it has a soporific virtue, and bread feeds because it has an alimentary quality. But the explanation is not so absurd. It says: "The beginning of civilization is marked by an intense legality; that legality is the very condition of its existence, the bond which ties it together; but that legality—that tendency to impose a settled customary yoke upon all men and all actions—if it goes on, kills out the variability implanted by nature, and makes different men and different ages facsimiles of other men and other ages, as we see them so often. Progress is only possible in those happy cases where the force of legality has gone far enough to bind the nation together, but not far enough to kill out all varieties and destroy nature's perpetual tendency to change." The point of the solution is not the invention of an imaginary agency, but an assignment of comparative magnitude to two known agencies.

III

This advantage is one of the greatest in early civilization —one of the facts which give a decisive turn to the battle of nations; but there are many others. A little perfection in *political institutions* may do it. Travelers have noticed that among savage tribes those seemed to answer best in which the monarchical power was most predominant, and those worst in which the "rule of many" was in its vigor. So long as war is the main business of nations, temporary despotism—despotism during the campaign—is indispensable. Macaulay* justly said that many an army has prospered under a bad commander, but no army has ever prospered under a "debating society"; that many-headed monster is then fatal. Despotism grows in the first societies, just as democracy grows in more modern societies; it is the government answering the primary need, and congenial to the whole spirit of the time. But despotism is unfavorable to the principle of variability, as all history shows. It tends to keep men in the customary stage of civilization; its very fitness for that age unfits it for the next. It prevents men from passing into the first age of progress—the *very* slow and *very* gradually improving age. Some "standing system" of semi-free discussion is as necessary to break the thick crust of custom and begin progress as it is in later ages to carry on progress when begun; probably it is even more necessary. And in the most progressive races we find it. I have spoken already of the Jewish prophets, the life of that nation, and the principle of all its growth. But a still more progressive race—that by which secular civilization was once created, by which it is now mainly administered—had a still better instrument of progression. "In the very earliest glimpses," says Mr. Freeman, "of

* [Thomas Babington Macaulay (1800–1869), influential English historian, essayist, and critic.—*Ed.*]

Teutonic political life, we find the monarchic, the aristocratic, and the democratic elements already clearly marked. There are leaders with or without the royal title; there are men of noble birth, whose noble birth (in whatever the original nobility may have consisted) entitles them to a pre-eminence in every way; but beyond these there is a free and armed people, in whom it is clear that the ultimate sovereignty resides. Small matters are decided by the chiefs alone; great matters are submitted by the chiefs to the assembled nation. Such a system is far more than Teutonic; it is a common Aryan possession; it is the constitution of the Homeric Achaians on earth and of the Homeric gods on Olympus."* Perhaps, and indeed probably, this constitution may be that of the primitive tribe which Romans left to go one way, and Greeks to go another, and Teutons to go a third. The tribe took it with them, as the English take the common law with them, because it was the one kind of polity which they could conceive and act upon; or it may be that the emigrants from the primitive Aryan stock only took with them a good aptitude—an excellent political nature, which similar circumstances in distant countries were afterwards to develop into like forms. But anyhow it is impossible not to trace the supremacy of Teutons, Greeks, and Romans in part to their common form of government. The contests of the assembly cherished the principle of change; the influence of the elders ensured sedateness and

* [Edward Augustus Freeman (1823–1892), historian and polemicist. This quotation is from the first volume of *The History of the Norman Conquest of England: Its Causes and Its Results*, five volumes (1867–1879) (Oxford: Oxford University Press, 1873), page 54.—*Ed.*]

preserved the mold of thought; and, in the best cases, military discipline was not impaired by freedom, though military intelligence was enhanced with the general intelligence. A Roman army was a free body, at its own choice governed by a peremptory despotism.

The *mixture of races* was often an advantage, too. Much as the old world believed in pure blood, it had very little of it. Most historic nations conquered prehistoric nations, and though they massacred many, they did not massacre all. They enslaved the subject men, and they married the subject women. No doubt the whole bond of early society was the bond of descent; no doubt it was essential to the notions of a new nation that it should have had common ancestors; the modern idea that vicinity of habitation is the natural cement of civil union would have been repelled as an impiety if it could have been conceived as an idea. But by one of those legal fictions which Sir Henry Maine describes so well, primitive nations contrived to do what they found convenient, as well as to adhere to what they fancied to be right. When they did not beget they *adopted*; they solemnly made believe that new persons were descended from the old stock, though everybody knew that in flesh and blood they were not. They made an artificial unity in default of a real unity; and what it is not easy to understand now, the sacred sentiment requiring unity of race was somehow satisfied: what was made did as well as what was born. Nations with this sort of maxims are not likely to have unity of race in the modern sense, and as a physiologist understands it. What sorts of unions improve the breed, and which are worse than both the father race and the mother, it is not very easy to say. The subject was reviewed by M. Quatrefages in an elaborate report upon the occasion of the French Exhibition, of all things in the world. M. Quatrefages* quotes from another writer the phrase that South America is a great laboratory of experiments in the mixture of races, and reviews the different results which different cases have shown. In South Carolina the mulatto race is not very prolific, whereas in Louisiana and Florida it decidedly is so. In Jamaica and in Java the mulatto cannot reproduce itself after the third generation; but on the continent of America, as everybody knows, the mixed race is now most numerous, and spreads generation after generation without impediment. Equally various likewise in various cases has been the fate of the mixed race between the white man and the native American; sometimes it prospers, sometimes it fails. And M. Quatrefages concludes his description thus: "En acceptant comme vraies toutes les observations qui tendent à faire admettre qu'il en sera autrement dans les localités dont j'ai parlé plus haut, quelle est la conclusion à tirer de faits aussi peu semblables? Evidemment, on est obligé de reconnaître que le développement de la race mulâtre est favorisé, retardé, ou empêché par des circonstances locales; en d'autres termes qu'il dépend des influences excercées par l'ensemble des conditions d'existence, par le *milieu.*"‡ By which I understand him to mean that the

* [Armand de Quatrefages (1810–1892), French anthropologist.—*Ed.*]

‡ ["In accepting as true all the observations which tend to make us admit that it will be otherwise in the places of which I've spoken above, what is the conclusion to draw from facts so little similar? Evidently, one is forced to recognize that the development of the mixed race is favored, held back, or impeded by local circumstances; in other words,

mixture of race sometimes brings out a form of character better suited than either parent form to the place and time; that in such cases, by a kind of natural selection, it dominates over both parents, and perhaps supplants both, whereas in other cases the mixed race is not as good then and there as other parent forms, and then it passes away soon and of itself.

Early in history the continual mixtures by conquest were just so many experiments in mixing races as are going on in South America now. New races wandered into new districts, and half killed, half mixed with the old races. And the result was doubtless as various and as difficult to account for then as now; sometimes the crossing answered, sometimes it failed. But when the mixture was at its best, it must have excelled both parents in that of which so much has been said; that is, variability, and consequently progressiveness. There is more life in mixed nations. France, for instance, is justly said to be the mean term between the Latin and the German races. A Norman, as you may see by looking at him, is of the north; a provençal is of the south, of all that there is most southern. You have in France Latin, Celtic, German, compounded in an infinite number of proportions: one as she is in feeling, she is various not only in the past history of her various provinces, but in their present temperaments. Like the Irish element and the Scotch element in the English House of Commons, the variety of French

that it depends on influences exercised by the whole of the condition of existence, by the environment." *Rapport sur les progrès de l'Anthropologie* (Paris: Hachette, 1867), page 445.—*Ed.*]

races contributes to the play of the polity; it gives a chance for fitting new things which otherwise there would not be. And early races must have wanted mixing more than modern races. It is said, in answer to the Jewish boast that "their race still prospers, though it is scattered and breeds in-and-in": "You prosper *because* you are so scattered; by acclimatization in various regions your nation has acquired singular elements of variety; it contains within itself the principle of variability which other nations must seek by intermarriage." In the beginning of things there was certainly no cosmopolitan race like the Jews; each race was a sort of "parish race," narrow in thought and bounded in range, and it wanted mixing accordingly.

But the mixture of races has a singular danger as well as a singular advantage in the early world. We know now the Anglo-Indian suspicion or contempt for "half-castes." The union of the Englishman and the Hindoo produces something not only between races, but *between moralities.* They have no inherited creed or plain place in the world; they have none of the fixed traditional sentiments which are the stays of human nature. In the early world many mixtures must have wrought many ruins; they must have destroyed what they could not replace—an inbred principle of discipline and of order. But if these unions of races did not work thus; if, for example, the two races were so near akin that their morals united as well as their breeds, if one race by its great numbers and prepotent organization so presided over the other as to take it up and assimilate it, and leave no separate remains of it, *then* the admixture was invaluable. It added to the probability of variability, and therefore of improvement; and if that improvement even in part took the military line, it might give the mixed and ameliorated state a steady advantage in the battle of nations, and a greater chance of lasting in the world.

Another mode in which one state acquires a superiority over competing states is by *provisional* institutions, if I may so call them. The most important of these—slavery —arises out of the same early conquest as the mixture of races. A slave is an unassimilated, an undigested atom; something which is in the body politic, but yet is hardly part of it. Slavery, too, has a bad name in the later world, and very justly. We connect it with gangs in chains, with laws which keep men ignorant, with laws that hinder families. But the evils which we have endured from slavery in recent ages must not blind us to, or make us forget, the great services that slavery rendered in early ages. There is a wonderful presumption in its favor; it is one of the institutions which, at a certain stage of growth, all nations in all countries choose and cleave to. "Slavery," says Aristotle, "exists by the law of nature," meaning that it was everywhere to be found—was a rudimentary universal point of polity.* "There are very many English colonies," said Edward Gibbon Wakefield, as late as 1848, "who would keep slaves at once if we would let them," and he was speaking not only of old colonies trained in slavery, and raised upon the products of it, but likewise of new colonies started by freemen, and which ought, one would think, to wish to contain freemen only.‡ But Wakefield knew what he was saying;

* [See Aristotle's discussion of slavery in *Politics* Book I, 1254a–1255a.—*Ed.*]
‡ [Edward Gibbon Wakefield (1796–1862), writer, social reformer, economist, and theorist of colonization. The passage

he was a careful observer of rough societies, and he had watched the minds of men in them. He had seen that *leisure* is the great need of early societies, and slaves only can give men leisure. All freemen in new countries must be pretty equal; every one has labor, and every one has land; capital, at least in agricultural countries (for pastoral countries are very different), is of little use; it cannot hire labor; the laborers go and work for themselves. There is a story often told of a great English capitalist who went out to Australia with a shipload of laborers and a carriage; his plan was that the laborers should build a house for him, and that he would keep his carriage, just as in England. But (so the story goes) he had to try to live in his carriage, for his laborers left him and went away to work for themselves.

In such countries there can be few gentlemen and no ladies. Refinement is only possible when leisure is possible; and slavery first makes it possible. It creates a set of persons born to work that others may not work, and not to think in order that others may think. The sort of originality which slavery gives is of the first practical advantage in early communities; and the repose it gives is a great artistic advantage when they come to be described in history. The patriarchs Abraham, Isaac, and Jacob could not have had the steady calm which marks them if

---

that Bagehot paraphrases here appears in *A View of the Art of Colonization, With Present Reference to the British Empire; In Letters Between a Statesman and a Colonist* (1849), *The Collected Works of Edward Gibbon Wakefield* (Auckland: Collins, 1969), edited by F. F. Lloyd Prichard, page 928.—Ed.]

they had themselves been teased and hurried about their flocks and herds. Refinement of feeling and repose of appearance have indeed no market value in the early bidding of nations; they do not tend to secure themselves a long future or any future. But originality in war does, and slave-owning nations, having time to think, are likely to be more shrewd in policy, and more crafty in strategy.

No doubt this momentary gain is bought at a ruinous after-cost. When other sources of leisure become possible, the one use of slavery is past. But all its evils remain, and even grow worse. "Retail" slavery—the slavery in which a master owns a few slaves, whom he well knows and daily sees—is not at all an intolerable state; the slaves of Abraham had no doubt a fair life, as things went in that day. But wholesale slavery, where men are but one of the investments of large capital, and where a great owner, so far from knowing each slave, can hardly tell how many gangs of them he works, is an abominable state. This is the slavery which has made the name revolting to the best minds, and has nearly rooted the thing out of the best of the world. There is no out-of-the-way marvel in this. The whole history of civilization is strewn with creeds and institutions which were invaluable at first, and deadly afterwards. Progress would not have been the rarity it is if the early food had not been the late poison. A full examination of these provisional institutions would need half a volume, and would be out of place and useless here. Venerable oligarchy, august monarchy, are two that would alone need large chapters. But the sole point here necessary is to say that such preliminary forms and feelings at first often bring many graces and many refinements, and often tend to secure them by the preservative military virtue.

There are cases in which some step in *intellectual* progress gives an early society some gain in war; more obvious cases are when some kind of *moral* quality gives some such gain. War both needs and generates certain virtues; not the highest, but what may be called the preliminary virtues, as valor, veracity, the spirit of obedience, the habit of discipline. Any of these, and of others like them, when possessed by a nation, and no matter how generated, will give them a military advantage, and make them more likely to *stay* in the race of nations. The Romans probably had as much of these efficacious virtues as any race of the ancient world—perhaps as much as any race in the modern world too. And the success of the nations which possess these martial virtues has been the great means by which their continuance has been secured in the world, and the destruction of the opposite vices ensured also. Conquest is the missionary of valor, and the hard impact of military virtues beats meanness out of the world.

In the last century it would have sounded strange to speak, as I am going to speak, of the military advantage of *religion*. Such an idea would have been opposed to ruling prejudices, and would hardly have escaped philosophical ridicule. But the notion is but a commonplace in our day, for a man of genius has made it his own. Mr. Carlyle's books are deformed by phrases like "infinities" and "verities," and altogether are full of faults, which attract the very young, and deter all that are older. In spite of his great genius, after a long life of writing, it is a question still whether even a single work of his can take a lasting place in high literature. There is a want of sanity in their manner which throws a suspicion on their substance (though it is often profound); and he brandishes one or two fallacies, of which he has himself a high notion, but which plain people will always detect and deride. But whatever may be the fate of his fame, Mr. Carlyle has taught the present generation many lessons, and one of these is that "God-fearing" armies are the best armies. Before his time people laughed at Cromwell's saying: "Trust in God, and keep your powder dry." But we now know that the trust was of as much use as the powder, if not of more. That high concentration of steady feeling makes men dare everything and do anything.

This subject would run to an infinite extent if anyone were competent to handle it. Those kinds of morals and that kind of religion which tend to make the firmest and most effectual character are sure to prevail, all else being the same; and creeds or systems that conduce to a soft limp mind tend to perish, except some hard extrinsic force keep them alive. Thus Epicureanism never prospered at Rome, but Stoicism did; the stiff, serious character of the great prevailing nation was attracted by what seemed a confirming creed, and deterred by what looked like a relaxing creed. The inspiriting doctrines fell upon the ardent character, and so confirmed its energy. Strong beliefs win strong men, and then make them stronger. Such is no doubt one cause why Monotheism tends to prevail over Polytheism; it produces a higher, steadier character, calmed and concentrated by a great single object; it is not confused by competing rites, or distracted by miscellaneous deities. Polytheism is religion *in commission,* and it is weak accordingly. But it will be said the Jews, who were monotheist, were conquered by the Romans, who were polytheist. Yes, it must be answered, because the Romans had other gifts; they had a capacity for politics, a habit of discipline, and of these the Jews had not the least. The religious advantage *was* an advantage, but it was counter weighed.

No one should be surprised at the prominence given to war. We are dealing with early ages; nation-*making* is the occupation of man in these ages, and it is war that makes nations. Nation-*changing* comes afterwards, and is mostly effected by peaceful revolution, though even then war, too, plays its part. The idea of an indestructible nation is a modern idea; in early ages all nations were destructible, and the further we go back, the more incessant was the work of destruction. The internal decoration of nations is a sort of secondary process, which succeeds when the main forces that create nations have principally done their work. We have here been concerned with the political scaffolding; it will be the task of other papers to trace the process of political finishing and building. The nicer play of finer forces may then require more pleasing thoughts than the fierce fights of early ages can ever suggest. It belongs to the idea of progress that beginnings can never seem attractive to those who live far on; the price of improvement is that the unimproved will always look degraded.

But how far are the strongest nations really the best nations? how far is excellence in war a criterion of other excellence? I cannot answer this now fully, but three or four considerations are very plain. War, as I have said, nourishes the "preliminary" virtues, and this is almost as much as to say that there are virtues which it does not nourish. All which may be called "grace" as well as virtue it does not nourish; humanity, charity, a nice sense of the rights of others, it certainly does not foster. The insensibility to human suffering, which is so striking a fact in the world as it stood when history first reveals it, is doubtless due to the warlike origin of the old civilization. Bred in war, and nursed in war, it could not revolt from the things of war, and one of the principal of these is human pain. Since war has ceased to be the moving force in the world, men have become more tender one to another, and shrink from what they used to inflict without caring; and this not so much because men are improved (which may or may not be in various cases), but because they have no longer the daily habit of war— have no longer formed their notions upon war, and therefore are guided by thoughts and feelings which soldiers as such—soldiers educated simply by their trade are too hard to understand.

Very like this is the contempt for physical weakness and for women which marks early society too. The noncombatant population is sure to fare ill during the ages of combat. But these defects, too, are cured or lessened; women have now marvelous means of winning their way in the world; and mind without muscle has far greater force than muscle without mind. These are some of the after-changes in the interior of nations, of which the causes must be scrutinized, and I now mention them only to bring out how many softer growths have now half-hidden the old and harsh civilization which war made.

But it is very dubious whether the spirit of war does not still color our morality far too much. Metaphors from law and metaphors from war make most of our current moral phrases, and a nice examination would easily explain that both rather vitiate what both often illustrate. The military habit makes man think far too much of definite action, and far too little of brooding meditation. Life is not a set campaign, but an irregular work, and the main forces in it are not overt resolutions, but latent and half-involuntary promptings. The mistake of military ethics is to exaggerate the conception of discipline, and so to present the moral force of the will in a barer form than it ever ought to take. Military morals can direct the axe to cut down the tree, but it knows nothing of the quiet force by which the forest grows.

What has been said is enough, I hope, to bring out that there are many qualities and many institutions of the most various sort which give nations an advantage in military competition; that most of these and most warlike qualities tend principally to good; that the constant winning of these favored competitors is the particular mode by which the best qualities wanted in elementary civilization are propagated and preserved.

3

Nation-making

I

IN THE last essay I endeavored to show that in the early age of man—the "fighting age" I called it—there was a considerable, though not certain, tendency towards progress. The best nations conquered the worst; by the possession of one advantage or another the best competitor overcame the inferior competitor. So long as there was continual fighting there was a likelihood of improvement in martial virtues, and in early times many virtues are really "martial"—that is, tend to success in war—which in later times we do not think of so calling, because the original usefulness is hid by their later usefulness. We judge of them by the present effects, not by their first. The love of law, for example, is a virtue which no one now would call martial, yet in early times it disciplined nations, and the disciplined nations won. The gift of "conservative innovation"—the gift of *matching* new institutions to old—is not nowadays a warlike virtue, yet the Romans owed much of their success to it. Alone among ancient nations they had the deference to usage which combines nations, and the partial permission of selected change which improves nations; and therefore they succeeded. Just so in most cases, all through the earliest times, martial merit is a token of real merit: the nation that wins is the nation that ought to win. The simple virtues of such ages mostly make a man a soldier if they make him anything. No doubt the brute force of number may be too potent even then (as so often it is afterwards): civilization may be thrown back by the conquest of many very rude men over a few less rude men. But the first elements of civilization are great military advantages, and, roughly, it is a rule of the first times that you can infer merit from conquest, and that progress is promoted by the competitive examination of constant war.

This principle explains at once why the "protected" regions of the world—the interior of continents like Africa, outlying islands like Australia or New Zealand— are of necessity backward. They are still in the preparatory school; they have not been taken on class by class, as No. II, being a little better, routed and effaced No. I; and as No. III, being a little better still, routed and effaced No. II. And it explains why western Europe was early in advance of other countries, because there the contest of races was exceedingly severe. Unlike most regions, it was a tempting part of the world, and yet not a corrupting part; those who did not possess it wanted it, and those who had it, not being enervated, could struggle hard to keep it. The conflict of nations is at first a main force in the improvement of nations.

But what *are* nations? What are these groups which are so familiar to us, and yet, if we stop to think, so strange; which are as old as history; which Herodotus found in almost as great numbers and with quite as marked distinctions as we see them now? What breaks the human race up into fragments so unlike one another, and yet each in its interior so monotonous? The question is most puzzling, though the fact is so familiar, and I would not venture to say that I can answer it completely, though I can advance some considerations which, as it seems to me, go a certain way towards answering it. Perhaps these same considerations throw some light, too, on the further and still more interesting question why some few nations progress, and why the greater part do not.

Of course at first all such distinctions of nation and nation were explained by original diversity of race. They *are* dissimilar, it was said, because they were created dissimilar. But in most cases this easy supposition will not do its work. You cannot (consistently with plain facts) imagine enough original races to make it tenable. Some half-dozen or more great families of men may or may not have been descended from separate first stocks, but subvarieties have certainly not so descended. You may argue, rightly or wrongly, that all Aryan nations are of a single or peculiar origin, just as it was long believed that all Greek-speaking nations were of one such stock. But you will not be listened to if you say that there were one Adam and Eve for Sparta, and another Adam and Eve for Athens. All Greeks are evidently of one origin, but within the limits of the Greek family, as of all other families, there is some contrast-making force which causes city to be unlike city, and tribe unlike tribe.

Certainly, too, nations did not originate by simple natural selection, as wild varieties of animals (I do not speak now of species) no doubt arise in nature. Natural selection means the preservation of those individuals which struggle best with the forces that oppose their race. But you could not show that the natural obstacles opposing human life much differed between Sparta and Athens, or indeed between Rome and Athens; and yet Spartans, Athenians, and Romans differ essentially. Old writers fancied (and it was a very natural idea) that the direct effect of climate, or rather of land, sea, and air, and the sum total of physical conditions varied man from man, and changed race to race. But experience refutes this. The English immigrant lives in the same climate as the Australian or Tasmanian, but he has not become like those races; nor will a thousand years, in most respects, make him like them. The Papuan and the Malay, as Mr. Wallace* finds, live now, and have lived for ages, side by side in the same tropical regions, with every sort of diversity. Even in animals his researches show, as by an object-lesson, that the direct efficacy of physical conditions is overrated. "Borneo," he says,

> closely resembles New Guinea, not only in its vast size and freedom from volcanoes, but in its variety of geological structure, its uniformity of climate, and the general aspect of the forest vegetation that clothes its surface. The Moluccas are the counterpart of the Philippines in their volcanic structure, their extreme fertility, their luxuriant forests, and their frequent earthquakes; and Bali, the east end of Java, has a climate almost as arid as that of Timor. Yet between these corresponding groups of islands, constructed, as it were, after the same pattern, subjected to the same

* [Alfred Russel Wallace (1823–1913), English naturalist who formulated a theory of evolution similar to Darwin's. The following quotation appears in *The Malay Archipelago: The Land of the Orang-utan and the Bird of Paradise* (London: Macmillan, 1922), pages 12–13.—Ed.]

climate, and bathed by the same oceans, there exists the greatest possible contrast, when we compare their animal productions. Nowhere does the ancient doctrine—that differences or similarities in the various forms of life that inhabit different countries are due to corresponding physical differences or similarities in the countries themselves—meet with so direct and palpable a contradiction. Borneo and New Guinea, as alike physically as two distinct countries can be, are zoologically as wide as the poles asunder; while Australia, with its dry winds, its open plains, its stony deserts, and its temperate climate, yet produces birds and quadrupeds which are closely related to those inhabiting the hot, damp, luxuriant forests which everywhere clothe the plains and mountains of New Guinea.

That is, we have like living things in the most dissimilar situations, and unlike living things in the most similar ones. And though some of Mr. Wallace's speculations on ethnology may be doubtful, no one doubts that in the archipelago he has studied so well, as often elsewhere in the world, though rarely with such marked emphasis, we find like men in contrasted places, and unlike men in resembling places. Climate is clearly not *the* force which makes nations, for it does not always make them, and they are often made without it.

The problem of "nation-making"—that is, the explanation of the origin of nations such as we now see them, and such as in historical times they have always been—cannot, as it seems to me, be solved without separating it into two: one, the making of broadly marked races, such as the Negro, or the red man, or the European; and the second, that of making the minor distinctions, such as the distinction between Spartan and Athenian, or between Scotchman and Englishman. Nations, as we see them, are (if my arguments prove true) the produce of two great forces: one the race-making force which, whatever it was, acted in antiquity, and has now wholly, or almost, given over acting; and the other the nation-making force, properly so called, which is acting now as much as it ever acted, and creating as much as it ever created.

The strongest light on the great causes which have formed and are forming nations is thrown by the smaller causes which are altering nations. The way in which nations change, generation after generation, is exceedingly curious, and the change occasionally happens when it is very hard to account for. Something seems to steal over society, say of the Regency time as compared with that of the present Queen. If we read of life at Windsor (at the cottage now pulled down), or of Bond Street as it was in the days of the Loungers (an extinct race), or of St. James's Street as it was when Mr. Fox* and his party tried to make "political capital" out of the dissipation of an heir apparent, we seem to be reading not of the places we know so well, but of very distant and unlike localities. Or let anyone think how little is the external change in England between the age of Elizabeth and the age of Anne compared with the national change. How few were the alterations in physical condition, how few (if any) the scientific inventions affecting human life which the later period possessed, but the earlier did not! How hard it is to say what has caused the change in the people! And yet how total is the contrast, at least at first sight! In passing

---

* [Charles James Fox (1749–1806), British Whig politician and orator.—*Ed.*]

from Bacon to Addison, from Shakespeare to Pope, we seem to pass into a new world.

In the first of these essays I spoke of the mode in which the literary change happens, and I recur to it because, literature being narrower and more definite than life, a change in the less serves as a model and illustration of the change in the greater. Some writer, as was explained, not necessarily a very excellent writer or a remembered one, hit on something which suited the public taste: he went on writing, and others imitated him, and they so accustomed their readers to that style that they would bear nothing else. Those readers who did not like it were driven to the works of other ages and other countries— had to despise the "trash of the day," as they would call it. The age of Anne patronized Steele, the beginner of the essay, and Addison, its perfecter, and it neglected writings in a wholly discordant key. I have heard that the founder of *The Times* was asked how all the articles in *The Times* came to seem to be written by one man, and that he replied: "Oh, there is always some one best contributor, and all the rest copy." And this is doubtless the true account of the manner in which a certain trade mark, a curious and indefinable unity, settles on every newspaper. Perhaps it would be possible to name the men who a few years since created the *Saturday Review* style, now imitated by another and a younger race. But when the style of a periodical is once formed, the continuance of it is preserved by a much more despotic impulse than the tendency to imitation—by the self-interest of the editor, who acts as *trustee*, if I may say so, for the subscribers. The regular buyers of a periodical want to read what they have been used to read—the same sort of thought, the same sort of words. The editor sees that they get that sort. He selects the suitable, the conforming articles, and he rejects the nonconforming. What the editor does in the case of a periodical, the readers do in the case of literature in general. They patronize one thing and reject the rest.

Of course there was always some reason (if we only could find it) which gave the prominence in each age to some particular winning literature. There always is some reason why the fashion of female dress is what it is. But just as in the case of dress we know that nowadays the determining cause is very much of an accident, so in the case of literary fashion, the origin is a good deal of an accident. What the milliners of Paris, or the *demi-monde* of Paris, enjoin our English ladies is (I suppose) a good deal chance; but as soon as it is decreed, those whom it suits and those whom it does not all wear it. The imitative propensity at once ensures uniformity; and "that horrid thing we wore last year" (as the phrase may go) is soon nowhere to be seen. Just so a literary fashion spreads, though I am far from saying with equal primitive unreasonableness—a literary taste always begins on some decent reason, but once started, it is propagated as a fashion in dress is propagated; even those who do not like it read it because it is there, and because nothing else is easily to be found.

The same patronage of favored forms, and persecution of disliked forms, are the main causes too, I believe, which change national character. Some one attractive type catches the eye, so to speak, of the nation, or a part of the nation, as servants catch the gait of their masters, or as mobile girls come home speaking the special words and acting the little gestures of each family whom they may have been visiting. I do not know if many of my readers happen to have read Father Newman's celebrated sermon, "Personal Influence the Means of Propagating the Truth";* if not, I strongly recommend them to do so. They will there see the opinion of a great practical leader of men, of one who has led very many where they little thought of going, as to the mode in which they are to be led; and what he says, put shortly and simply, and taken out of his delicate language, is but this—that men are guided by *type*, not by argument; that some winning instance must be set up before them, or the sermon will be vain, and the doctrine will not spread. I do not want to illustrate this matter from religious history, for I should be led far from my purpose, and after all I can but teach the commonplace that it is the life of teachers which *is catching*, not their tenets. And again, in political matters, how quickly a leading statesman can change the tone of the community! We are most of us earnest with Mr. Gladstone; we were most of us *not* so earnest in the time of Lord Palmerston.‡ The change is what everyone feels, though no one can define it. Each predominant mind calls out a corresponding sentiment in the country: most feel it a little. Those who feel it much express it much; those who feel it excessively express it excessively; those who dissent are silent, or unheard.

---

* [John Henry Newman (1801–1890), influential English chruchman and writer who converted to Roman Catholicism (1845) and rose to become a cardinal. The sermon Bagehot refers to is available, e.g., in *Fifteen Sermons Preached Before the University of Oxford* (London: Longmans, Green, and Co., 1896), pages 75–98.—*Ed.*]

‡ [Henry John Temple, 3rd Viscount Palmerston (1784–1865), British statesman, prime minister 1855–1858, 1859–1865. —*Ed.*]

After such great matters as religion and politics, it may seem trifling to illustrate the subject from little boys. But it is not trifling. The bane of philosophy is pomposity: people will not see that small things are the miniatures of greater, and it seems a loss of abstract dignity to freshen their minds by object-lessons from what they know. But every boarding-school changes as a nation changes. Most of us may remember thinking: "How odd it is that this 'half' should be so unlike last 'half': now we never go out of bounds, last half we were always going; now we play rounders, then we played prisoner's base"; and so through all the easy life of that time. In fact, some ruling spirits, some one or two ascendant boys, had left, one or two others had come—and so all was changed. The models were changed, and the copies changed; a different thing was praised, and a different thing bullied. A curious case of the same tendency was noticed to me only lately. A friend of mine—a Liberal Conservative—addressed a meeting of working men at Leeds and was much pleased at finding his characteristic, and perhaps refined points, both apprehended and applauded. "But then," as he narrated, "up rose a blatant Radical who said the very opposite things, and the working men cheered him too, and quite equally." He was puzzled to account for so rapid a change. But the mass of the meeting was no doubt nearly neutral, and, if set going, quite ready to applaud any good words without much thinking. The ringleaders changed. The radical tailor started the radical cheer; the more moderate shoemaker started the moderate cheer; and the great bulk followed suit. Only a few in each case were silent, and an absolute contrast was in ten minutes presented by the same elements.

The truth is that the propensity of man to imitate what

is before him is one of the strongest parts of his nature.
And one sign of it is the great pain which we feel when
our imitation has been unsuccessful. There is a cynical
doctrine that most men would rather be accused of wick-
edness than of *gaucherie*. And this is but another way of
saying that the bad copying of predominant manners is
felt to be more of a disgrace than common consideration
would account for its being, since *gaucherie* in all but extravagant cases is not an offence against religion or
morals, but is simply bad imitation.

We must not think that this imitation is voluntary, or
even conscious. On the contrary, it has its seat mainly in
very obscure parts of the mind, whose notions, so far
from having been consciously produced, are hardly felt to
exist; so far from being conceived beforehand, are not
even felt at the time. The main seat of the imitative part
of our nature is our belief, and the causes predisposing us
to believe this, or disinclining us to believe that, are
among the obscurest parts of our nature. But as to the
imitative nature of credulity there can be no doubt. In
*Eothen** there is a capital description of how every sort of
European resident in the East, even the shrewd merchant
and "the post-captain," with his bright, wakeful eyes of
commerce, comes soon to believe in witchcraft, and to
assure you, in confidence, that there "really is something
in it." He has never seen anything convincing himself, but

---

* [*Eothen, or, Traces of Travel Brought Home from the East* is
a classic travel book, published anonymously in 1844 by the
English writer Alexander William Kinglake (1809–1891). In
the edition introduced by V. S. Pritchett (Lincoln: University
of Nebraska Press, 1970), the passage Bagehot refers to may
be found on pages 130–131.—*Ed.*]

he has seen those who have seen those who have seen those who have seen. In fact, he has lived in an atmosphere of infectious belief, and he has inhaled it. Scarcely anyone can help yielding to the current infatuations of his sect or party. For a short time, say some fortnight—he is resolute; he argues and objects; but, day by day, the poison thrives, and reason wanes. What he hears from his friends, what he reads in the party organ, produces its effect. The plain, palpable conclusion which everyone around him believes has an influence yet greater and more subtle; that conclusion seems so solid and unmistakable; his own good arguments get daily more and more like a dream. Soon the gravest sage shares the folly of the party with which he acts and the sect with which he worships.

In true metaphysics I believe that, contrary to common opinion, unbelief far oftener needs a reason and requires an effort than belief. Naturally, and if man were made according to the pattern of the logicians, he would say: "When I see a valid argument I will believe, and till I see such argument I will not believe." But, in fact, every idea vividly before us soon appears to us to be true, unless we keep up our perceptions of the arguments which prove it untrue, and voluntarily coerce our minds to remember its falsehood. "All clear ideas are true," was for ages a philosophical maxim, and though no maxim can be more unsound, none can be more exactly conformable to ordinary human nature. The child resolutely accepts every idea which passes through its brain as true; it has no distinct conception of an idea which is strong, bright, and permanent, but which is false too. The mere presentation of an idea, unless we are careful about it, or unless there is within some unusual resistance, makes us believe it;

and this is why the belief of others adds to our belief so quickly, for no ideas seem so very clear as those inculcated on us from every side.

The grave part of mankind are quite as liable to these imitated beliefs as the frivolous part. The belief of the money-market, which is mainly composed of grave people, is as imitative as any belief. You will find one day everyone enterprising, enthusiastic, vigorous, eager to buy, and eager to order; in a week or so you will find almost the whole society depressed, anxious, and wanting to sell. If you examine the reasons for the activity, or for the inactivity, or for the change, you will hardly be able to trace them at all, and as far as you can trace them, they are of little force. In fact, these opinions were not formed by reason, but by mimicry. Something happened that looked a little good, on which eager sanguine men talked loudly, and common people caught their tone. A little while afterwards, and when people were tired of talking thus, something also happened looking a little bad, on which the dismal, anxious people began, and all the rest followed their words. And in both cases an avowed dissentient is set down as "crotchety." "If you want," said Swift,* "to gain the reputation of a sensible man, you should be of the opinion of the person with whom for the time being you are conversing." There is much quiet intellectual persecution among "reasonable" men; a cautious person hesitates before he tells them anything new, for if he gets a name for such things he will be called "flighty," and in times of decision he will not be attended to.

---

* [Jonathan Swift (1667–1745), Anglo-Irish poet, satirist, and churchman.—*Ed.*]

In this way the infection of imitation catches men in their most inward and intellectual part—their creed. But it also invades men—by the most bodily part of the mind, so to speak—the link between soul and body—the manner. No one needs to have this explained; we all know how a kind of subtle influence makes us imitate or try to imitate the manner of those around us. To conform to the fashion of Rome—whatever the fashion may be, and whatever Rome we may for the time be at—is among the most obvious needs of human nature. But what is not so obvious, though as certain, is that the influence of the imitation goes deep as well as extends wide. "The matter," as Wordsworth says, "of style very much comes out of the manner." If you will endeavor to write an imitation of the thoughts of Swift in a copy of the style of Addison, you will find that not only is it hard to write Addison's style, from its intrinsic excellence, but also that the more you approach to it the more you lose the thought of Swift. The eager passion of the meaning beats upon the mild drapery of the words. So you could not express the plain thoughts of an Englishman in the grand manner of a Spaniard. Insensibly, and as by a sort of magic, the kind of manner which a man catches eats into him and makes him in the end what at first he only seems.

This is the principal mode in which the greatest minds of an age produce their effect. They set the tone which others take, and the fashion which others use. There is an odd idea that those who take what is called a "scientific view" of history need rate lightly the influence of individual character. It would be as reasonable to say that those who take a scientific view of nature need think little of the influence of the sun. On the scientific view a great man is a great new cause (compounded or not out of other causes, for I do not here, or elsewhere in these papers, raise the question of free will), but, anyhow, new in all its effects, and all its results. Great models for good and evil sometimes appear among men, who follow them either to improvement or degradation.

I am, I know, very long and tedious in setting out this; but I want to bring home to others what every new observation of society brings more and more freshly to myself—that this unconscious imitation and encouragement of appreciated character, and this equally unconscious shrinking from and persecution of disliked character, is the main force which molds and fashions men in society as we now see it. Soon I shall try to show that the more acknowledged causes, such as change of climate, alteration of political institutions, progress of science, act principally through this cause; that they change the object of imitation and the object of avoidance, and so work their effect. But first I must speak of the origin of nations—of nation-making as one may call it —the proper subject of this paper.

The process of nation-making is one of which we have obvious examples in the most recent times, and which is going on now. The most simple example is the foundation of the first State of America, say New England, which has such a marked and such a deep national character. A great number of persons agreeing in fundamental disposition, agreeing in religion, agreeing in politics, form a separate settlement; they exaggerate their own disposition, teach their own creed, set up their favorite government; they discourage all other dispositions, persecute other beliefs, forbid other forms or habits of government. Of course a nation so made will have a separate stamp and mark. The original settlers began of one type; they sedulously imitated it; and (though other causes have intervened and disturbed it) the necessary operation of the principles of inheritance has transmitted many original traits still unaltered, and has left an entire New England character—in no respect unaffected by its first character.

This case is well known, but it is not so that the same process, in a weaker shape, is going on in America now. Congeniality of sentiment is a reason of selection, and a bond of cohesion in the "West" at present. Competent observers say that townships grow up there by each place taking its own religion, its own manners, and its own ways. Those who have these morals and that religion go to that place, and stay there; and those who have not these morals and that religion either settle elsewhere at first, or soon pass on. The days of colonization by sudden "swarms" of like creed are almost over, but a less visible process of attraction by similar faith over similar is still in vigor, and very likely to continue.

And in cases where this principle does not operate, all new settlements, being formed of "emigrants," are sure to be composed of rather restless people, mainly. The stay-at-home people are not to be found there, and these are the quiet, easy people. A new settlement voluntarily formed (for of old times, when people were expelled by terror, I am not speaking) is sure to have in it much more than the ordinary proportion of active men, and much less than the ordinary proportion of inactive; and this accounts for a large part, though not perhaps all, of the difference between the English in England and the English in Australia.

The causes which formed New England in recent times cannot be conceived as acting much upon mankind in their infancy. Society is not then formed upon a "voluntary system" but upon an involuntary. A man in early ages is born to a certain obedience and cannot extricate himself from an inherited government. Society then is made up, not of individuals, but of families; creeds then descend by inheritance in those families. Lord Melbourne* once incurred the ridicule of philosophers by saying he should adhere to the English Church *because* it was the religion of his fathers. The philosophers, of course, said that a man's fathers' believing anything was no reason for his believing it unless it was true. But Lord Melbourne was only uttering out of season, and in a modern time, one of the most firm and accepted maxims of old times. A secession on religious grounds of isolated Romans to sail beyond sea would have seemed to the ancient Romans an impossibility. In still ruder ages the religion of savages is a thing too feeble to create a schism or to found a community. We are dealing with people capable of history when we speak of great ideas, not with prehistoric flint-men or the present savages. But though under very different forms, the same essential causes—the imitation of preferred characters and the elimination of detested characters were at work in the oldest times, and are at work among rude men now. Strong as the propensity to imitation is among civilized men, we must conceive it as an impulse of which their minds have been partially denuded. Like the far-seeing sight, the infallible hearing, the magical scent of the savage, it is a half-lost power. It was strongest in ancient times, and *is* strongest in uncivilized regions.

This extreme propensity to imitation is one great

* [William Lamb, 2nd Viscount Melbourne (1779–1848), prime minister 1834, 1835–1849, 1839–1841.—*Ed.*]

reason of the amazing sameness which every observer notices in savage nations. When you have seen one Fuegian, you have seen all Fuegians—one Tasmanian, all Tasmanians. The higher savages, as the New Zealanders, are less uniform; they have more of the varied and compact structure of civilized nations, because in other respects they are more civilized. They have greater mental capacity—larger stores of inward thought. But much of the same monotonous nature clings to them too. A savage tribe resembles a herd of gregarious beasts; where the leader goes they go too; they copy blindly his habits, and thus soon become that which he already is. For not only the tendency, but also the power to imitate is stronger in savages than civilized men. Savages copy quicker, and they copy better. Children, in the same way, are born mimics; they cannot help imitating what comes before them. There is nothing in their minds to resist the propensity to copy. Every educated man has a large inward supply of ideas to which he can retire, and in which he can escape from or alleviate unpleasant outward objects. But a savage or a child has no resource. The external movements before it are its very life; it lives by what it sees and hears. Uneducated people in civilized nations have vestiges of the same condition. If you send a housemaid and a philosopher to a foreign country of which neither knows the language, the chances are that the housemaid will catch it before the philosopher. He has something else to do; he can live in his own thoughts. But unless she can imitate the utterances, she is lost; she has no life till she can join in the chatter of the kitchen. The propensity to mimicry, and the power of mimicry, are mostly strongest in those who have least abstract minds. The most wonderful examples of imitation in the world are perhaps the imitations of civilized men by savages in the use of martial weapons. They learn the *knack*, as sportsmen call it, with inconceivable rapidity. A North American Indian—an Australian even—can shoot as well as any white man. Here the motive is at its maximum, as well as the innate power. Every savage cares more for the power of killing than for any other power.

The persecuting tendency of all savages, and, indeed, of all ignorant people, is even more striking than their imitative tendency. No barbarian can bear to see one of his nation deviate from the old barbarous customs and usages of their tribe. Very commonly all the tribe would expect a punishment from the gods if any one of them refrained from what was old, or began what was new. In modern times and in cultivated countries we regard each person as responsible only for his own actions, and do not believe, or think of believing, that the misconduct of others can bring guilt on them. Guilt to us is an individual taint consequent on choice and cleaving to the chooser. But in early ages the act of one member of the tribe is conceived to make all the tribe impious, to offend its peculiar god, to expose all the tribe to penalties from heaven. There is no "limited liability" in the political notions of that time. The early tribe or nation is a religious partnership, on which a rash member by a sudden impiety may bring utter ruin. If the state is conceived thus, toleration becomes wicked. A permitted deviation from the transmitted ordinances becomes simply folly. It is a sacrifice of the happiness of the greatest number. It is allowing one individual, for a moment's pleasure or a stupid whim, to bring terrible and irretrievable calamity upon all. No one will ever understand even Athenian history who forgets this idea of the old world, though

Athens was, in comparison with others, a rational and skeptical place, ready for new views, and free from old prejudices. When the street statues of Hermes were mutilated, all the Athenians were frightened and furious; they thought that they should *all* be ruined because some *one* had mutilated a god's image and so offended him. Almost every detail of life in the classical times—the times when real history opens—was invested with a religious sanction; a sacred ritual regulated human action; whether it was called "law" or not, much of it was older than the word "law"; it was part of an ancient usage conceived as emanating from a superhuman authority, and not to be transgressed without risk of punishment by more than mortal power. There was such a *solidarité* then between citizens that each might be led to persecute the other for fear of harm to himself.

It may be said that these two tendencies of the early world—that to persecution and that to imitation—must conflict; that the imitative impulse would lead men to copy what is new, and that persecution by traditional habit would prevent their copying it. But in practice the two tendencies cooperate. There is a strong tendency to copy the most common thing, and that common thing is the old habit. Daily imitation is far oftenest a conservative force, for the most frequent models are ancient. Of course, however, something new is necessary for every man and for every nation. We may wish, if we please, that tomorrow shall be like today, but it will not be like it. New forces will impinge upon us; new wind, new rain, and the light of another sun; and we must alter to meet them. But the persecuting habit and the imitative combine to ensure that the new thing shall be in the old fashion; it must be an alteration, but it shall contain as little of variety as possible. The imitative impulse tends to this, because men most easily imitate what their minds are best prepared for—what is like the old, yet with the inevitable minimum of alteration; what throws them least out of the old path, and puzzles least their minds. The doctrine of development means this—that in unavoidable changes men like the new doctrine which is most of a "preservative addition" to their old doctrines. The imitative and the persecuting tendencies make all change in early nations a kind of selective conservatism, for the most part keeping what is old, but annexing some new but like practice—an additional turret in the old style.

It is this process of adding suitable things and rejecting discordant things which has raised those scenes of strange manners which in every part of the world puzzle the civilized men who come upon them first. Like the old head-dress of mountain villages, they make the traveler think not so much whether they are good or whether they are bad as wonder how anyone could have come to think of them; to regard them as "monstrosities," which only some wild abnormal intellect could have hit upon. And wild and abnormal indeed would be that intellect if it were a single one at all. But in fact such manners are the growth of ages, like Roman law or the British Constitution. No one man—no one generation—could have thought of them—only a series of generations trained in the habits of the last and wanting something akin to such habits could have devised them. Savages *pet* their favorite habits, so to say, and preserve them as they do their favorite animals; ages are required, but at last a national character is formed by the confluence of congenial attractions and accordant detestations.

Another cause helps. In early states of civilization there

is a great mortality of infant life, and this is a kind of selection in itself—the child most fit to be a good Spartan is most likely to survive a Spartan childhood. The habits of the tribe are enforced on the child; if he is able to catch and copy them he lives; if he cannot he dies. The imitation which assimilates early nations continues through life, but it begins with suitable forms and acts on picked specimens. I suppose, too, that there is a kind of parental selection operating in the same way and probably tending to keep alive the same individuals. Those children which gratified their fathers and mothers most would be most tenderly treated by them, and have the best chance to live, and as a rough rule their favorites would be the children of most "promise"; that is to say, those who seemed most likely to be a credit to the tribe according to the leading tribal manners and the existing tribal tastes. The most gratifying child would be the best looked after, and the most gratifying would be the best specimen of the standard then and there raised up.

Even so, I think there will be a disinclination to attribute so marked, fixed, almost physical a thing as national character to causes so evanescent as the imitation of appreciated habit and the persecution of detested habit. But, after all, national character is but a name for a collection of habits more or less universal. And this imitation and this persecution in long generations have vast physical effects. The mind of the parent (as we speak) passes somehow to the body of the child. The transmitted "something" is more affected by habits than it is by anything else. In time an ingrained type is sure to be formed, and sure to be passed on if only the causes I have specified be fully in action and without impediment.

As I have said, I am not explaining the origin of races, but of nations, or, if you like, of, tribes. I fully admit that no imitation of predominant manners, or prohibitions of detested manners, will of themselves account for the broadest contrasts of human nature. Such means would no more make a Negro out of a Brahmin, or a red man out of an Englishman, than washing would change the spots of a leopard or the color of an Ethiopian. Some more potent causes must cooperate, or we should not have these enormous diversities. The minor causes I deal with made Greek to differ from Greek, but they did not make the Greek race. We cannot precisely mark the limit, but a limit there clearly is.

If we look at the earliest monuments of the human race, we find these race-characters as decided as the race-characters now. The earliest paintings or sculptures we anywhere have give us the present contrasts of dissimilar types as strongly as present observation. Within historical memory no such differences have been created as those between Negro and Greek, between Papuan and red Indian, between Eskimo and Goth. We start with cardinal diversities; we trace only minor modifications, and we only see minor modifications. And it is very hard to see how any number of such modifications could change man as he is in one race-type to man as he is in some other. Of this there are but two explanations; *one*, that these great types were originally separate creations, as they stand— that the Negro was made so, and the Greek made so. But this easy hypothesis of special creation has been tried so often, and has broken down so very often, that in no case, probably, do any great number of careful inquirers very firmly believe it. They may accept it provisionally, as the best hypothesis at present, but they feel about it as they cannot help feeling as to an army which has always been beaten; however strong it seems, they think it will be beaten again. What the other explanation is exactly I cannot pretend to say. Possibly as yet the data for a confident opinion are not before us. But by far the most plausible suggestion is that of Mr. Wallace, that these race-marks are living records of a time when the intellect of man was not as able as it is now to adapt his life and habits to change of region; that consequently early mortality in the first wanderers was beyond conception great; that only those (so to say) haphazard individuals throve who were born with a protected nature—that is, a nature suited to the climate and the country, fitted to use its advantages, shielded from its natural diseases. According to Mr. Wallace, the Negro is the remnant of the one variety of man who without more adaptiveness than then existed could live in interior Africa. Immigrants died off till they produced him or something like him, and so of the Eskimo or the American.

Any protective habit also struck out in such a time would have a far greater effect than it could afterwards. A gregarious tribe, whose leader was in some imitable respects adapted to the struggle for life, and which copied its leader, would have an enormous advantage in the struggle for life. It would be sure to win and live, for it would be coherent and adapted, whereas, in comparison, competing tribes would be incoherent and unadapted. And I suppose that in early times, when those bodies did not already contain the records and the traces of endless generations, any new habit would more easily fix its mark on the heritable element, and would be transmitted more easily and more certainly. In such an age, man being softer and more pliable, deeper race-marks would be more easily inscribed and would be more likely to continue legible.

But I have no pretense to speak on such matters; this paper, as I have so often explained, deals with nation-making and not with race-making. I assume a world of marked varieties of man, and only want to show how less marked contrasts would probably and naturally arise in each. Given large homogeneous populations, some Negro, some Mongolian, some Aryan, I have tried to prove how small contrasting groups would certainly spring up within each—some to last and some to perish. These are the eddies in each race-stream which vary its surface, and are sure to last till some new force changes the current. These minor varieties, too, would be infinitely compounded, not only with those of the same race, but with those of others. Since the beginning of man, stream has been a thousand times poured into stream—quick into sluggish, dark into pale—and eddies and waters have taken new shapes and new colors, affected by what went before, but not resembling it. And then on the fresh mass the old forces of composition and elimination again begin to act, and create over the new surface another world. "Motley was the wear" of the world when Herodotus first looked on it and described it to us, and thus, as it seems to me, were its varying colors produced.

If it be thought that I have made out that these forces of imitation and elimination be the main ones, or even at all powerful ones, in the formation of national character, it will follow that the effect of ordinary agencies upon that character will be more easy to understand than it often seems and is put down in books. We get a notion that a change of government or a change of climate acts

equally on the mass of a nation, and so are we puzzled—
at least, I have been puzzled—to conceive how it acts. But
such changes do not at first act equally on all people in
the nation. On many, for a very long time, they do not act
at all. But they bring out new qualities, and advertise the
effects of new habits. A change of climate, say from a
depressing to an invigorating one, so acts. Everybody
feels it a little, but the most active feel it exceedingly.
They labor and prosper, and their prosperity invites imitation. Just so with the contrary change, from an animating to a relaxing place—the naturally lazy look so
happy as they do nothing that the naturally active are
corrupted. The effect of any considerable change on a
nation is thus an intensifying and accumulating effect.
With its maximum power it acts on some prepared and
congenial individuals; in them it is seen to produce attractive results, and then the habits creating those results
are copied far and wide. And, as I believe, it is in this
simple but not quite obvious way that the process of
progress and of degradation may generally be seen to run.

4

Nation-making (continued)

A LL THEORIES as to the primitive man must be very uncertain. Granting the doctrine of evolution to be true, man must be held to have a common ancestor with the rest of the *primates*. But then we do not know what their common ancestor was like. If ever we are to have a distinct conception of him, it can only be after long years of future researches and the laborious accumulation of materials, scarcely the beginning of which now exists. But science has already done something for us. It cannot yet tell us our first ancestor, but it can tell us much of an ancestor very high up in the line of descent. We cannot get the least idea (even upon the full assumption of the theory of evolution) of the first man; but we can get a very tolerable idea of the paulo-prehistoric man, if I may so say—of man as he existed some short time (as we now reckon shortness), some ten thousand years, before history began. Investigators whose acuteness and diligence can hardly be surpassed—Sir John Lubbock and Mr. Tylor* are the chiefs among them—have collected so

* [Sir Edward Burnett Tylor (1832–1917), English anthropologist whose speciality was primitive religion.—*Ed.*]

much and explained so much that they have left a fairly vivid result.

That result is, or seems to me to be, if I may sum it up in my own words, that the modern prehistoric men— those of whom we have collected so many remains, and to whom are due the ancient, strange customs of historical nations (the fossil customs, we might call them, for very often they are stuck by themselves in real civilization, and have no more part in it than the fossils in the surrounding strata)—prehistoric men in this sense were "savages without the fixed habits of savages"; that is, that, like savages, they had strong passions and weak reason; that, like savages, they preferred short spasms of greedy pleasure to mild and equable enjoyment; that, like savages, they could not postpone the present to the future; that, like savages, their ingrained sense of morality was, to say the best of it, rudimentary and defective. But that, unlike present savages, they had not complex customs and singular customs, odd and seemingly inexplicable rules guiding all human life. And the reasons for these conclusions as to a race too ancient to leave a history, but not too ancient to have left memorials, are briefly these: First, that we cannot imagine a strong reason without attainments; and, plainly, prehistoric men had not attainments. They would never have lost them if they had. It is utterly incredible that whole races of men in the most distant parts of the world (capable of counting, for they quickly learn to count) should have lost the art of counting, if they had ever possessed it. It is incredible that whole races could lose the elements of common sense, the elementary knowledge as to things material and things mental—the Benjamin Franklin philosophy—if they had ever known it. Without some data the reasoning faculties of man cannot work. As Lord Bacon* said, the mind of man must "work upon stuff." And in the absence of the common knowledge which trains us in the elements of reason as far as we are trained, they had no "stuff." Even, therefore, if their passions were not absolutely stronger than ours, relatively they were stronger, for their reason was weaker than our reason. Again, it is certain that races of men capable of postponing the present to the future (even if such races were conceivable without an educated reason) would have had so huge an advantage in the struggles of nations that no others would have survived them. A single Australian tribe (really capable of such a habit, and really practicing it) would have conquered all Australia almost as the English have conquered it. Suppose a race of long-headed Scotchmen, even as ignorant as the Australians, and they would have got from Torres to Bass's Straits, no matter how fierce was the resistance of the other Australians. The whole territory would have been theirs and theirs only. We cannot imagine innumerable races to have lost, if they had once had it, the most useful of all habits of mind—the habit which would most ensure their victory in the incessant contests which, ever since they began, men have carried on with one another and with nature, the habit which in historical times has above any other received for its possession the victory in those contests. Thirdly, we may be sure that the morality of prehistoric man was as imperfect and as rudimentary as his reason. The same sort of arguments apply to a self-

* [Francis Bacon, 1st Baron Verulan and Viscount St. Albans (1561–1626), English essayist, courtier, scientist, and philosopher.—Ed.]

restraining morality of a high type as apply to a settled postponement of the present to the future upon grounds recommended by argument. Both are so involved in difficult intellectual ideas (and a high morality the more of the two) that it is all but impossible to conceive their existence among people who could not count more than five—who had only the grossest and simplest forms of language—who had no kind of writing or reading—who, as it has been roughly said, had "no pots and no pans"— who could indeed make a fire, but who could hardly do anything else—who could hardly command nature any further. Exactly also like a shrewd far-sightedness, a sound morality on elementary transactions is far too useful a gift to the human race ever to have been thoroughly lost when they had once attained it. But innumerable savages have lost all but completely many of the moral rules most conducive to tribal welfare. There are many savages who can hardly be said to care for human life— who have scarcely the family feelings—who are eager to kill all old people (their own parents included) as soon as they get old and become a burden—who have scarcely the sense of truth—who, probably from a constant tradition of terror, wish to conceal everything, and would (as observers say) "rather lie than not"—whose ideas of marriage are so vague and slight that the idea "communal marriage" (in which all the women of the tribe are common to all the men, and them only) has been invented to denote it. Now if we consider how cohesive and how fortifying to human societies are the love of truth, and the love of parents, and a stable marriage tie, how sure such feelings would be to make a tribe which possessed them wholly and soon victorious over tribes which were destitute of them, we shall begin to comprehend how unlikely it is that vast masses of tribes throughout the world should have lost all these moral helps to conquest, not to speak of others. If any reasoning is safe as to prehistoric man, the reasoning which imputes to him a deficient sense of morals is safe, for all the arguments suggested by all our late researches converge upon it, and concur in teaching it.

Nor on this point does the case rest wholly on recent investigations. Many years ago Mr. Jowett said that the classical religions bore relics of the "ages before morality." And this is only one of several cases in which that great thinker has proved by a chance expression that he had exhausted impending controversies years before they arrived, and had perceived more or less the conclusion at which the disputants would arrive long before the public issue was joined. There is no other explanation of such religions than this. We have but to open Mr. Gladstone's *Homer* in order to see with how intense an antipathy a really moral age would regard the gods and goddesses of Homer; how inconceivable it is that a really moral age should first have invented and then bowed down before them; how plain it is (when once explained) that they are antiquities, like an English court-suit, or a *stone* sacrificial knife, for no one would use such things as implements of ceremony except those who had inherited them from a past age, when there was nothing better.

Nor is there anything inconsistent with our present moral theories of whatever kind in so thinking about our ancestors. The intuitive theory of morality, which would be that naturally most opposed to it, has lately taken a new development. It is not now maintained that all men have the same amount of conscience. Indeed, only a most shallow disputant who did not understand even the plainest facts of human nature could ever have maintained it; if men differ in anything they differ in the fineness and the delicacy of their moral intuitions, however we may suppose those feelings to have been acquired. We need not go as far as savages to learn that lesson; we need only talk to the English poor or to our own servants and we shall be taught it very completely. The lower classes in civilized countries, like all classes in uncivilized countries, are clearly wanting in the nicer part of those feelings which, taken together, we call the *sense* of morality. All this an intuitionist who knows his case will now admit, but he will add that, though the amount of the moral sense may and does differ in different persons, yet that as far as it goes it is alike in all. He likens it to the intuition of number, in which some savages are so defective that they cannot really and easily count more than three. Yet as far as three his intuitions are the same as those of civilized people. Unquestionably if there are intuitions at all, the primary truths of number are such. There is a felt necessity in them if in anything, and it would be pedantry to say that any proposition of morals was *more* certain than that five and five make ten. The truths of arithmetic, intuitive or not, certainly cannot be acquired independently of experience nor can those of morals be so either. Unquestionably they were aroused in life and by experience, though after that comes the difficult and ancient controversy whether anything peculiar to them and not to be found in the other facts of life is superadded to them independently of experience out of the vigor of the mind itself. No intuitionist, therefore, fears to speak of the conscience of his prehistoric ancestor as imperfect, rudimentary, or hardly to be discerned, for he has to admit much the same so as to square his theory to plain modern facts, and that theory in the modern form may consistently be held along with them. Of course if an intuitionist can accept this conclusion as to prehistoric men, so assuredly may Mr. Spencer, who traces all morality back to our inherited experience of utility, or Mr. Darwin, who ascribes it to an inherited sympathy, or Mr. Mill,* who with characteristic courage undertakes to build up the whole moral nature of man with no help whatever either from ethical intuition or from physiological instinct. Indeed, of the everlasting questions, such as the reality of free will, or the nature of conscience, it is, as I have before explained, altogether inconsistent with the design of these papers to speak. They have been discussed ever since the history of discussion begins; human opinion is still divided, and most people still feel many difficulties in every suggested theory, and doubt if they have heard the last word of argument or the whole solution of the problem in any of them. In the interest of sound knowledge it is essential to narrow to the utmost the debatable territory; to see how many ascertained facts there are which are consistent with all theories, how many may, as foreign lawyers would phrase it, be equally held in *condominium* by them.

But though in these great characteristics there is reason to imagine that the prehistoric man—at least the sort of

---

* [Herbert Spencer (1820–1903), English philosopher, social thinker, and popularizer of "social Darwinism"; Charles Robert Darwin (1809–1882), the great English naturalist, first gave scientific grounding to the theory of organic evolution by means of natural selection; John Stuart Mill (1806–1873), English philosopher, social critic, and proponent of Utilitarianism.—*Ed.*]

prehistoric man I am treating of, the man some few thousand years before history began, and not at all, at least not necessarily, the primitive man—was identical with a modern savage, in another respect there is equal or greater reason to suppose that he was most unlike a modern savage. A modern savage is anything but the simple being which philosophers of the eighteenth century imagined him to be; on the contrary, his life is twisted into a thousand curious habits; his reason is darkened by a thousand strange prejudices; his feelings are frightened by a thousand cruel superstitions. The whole mind of a modern savage is, so to say, *tattooed* over with monstrous images; there is not a smooth place anywhere about it. But there is no reason to suppose the minds of prehistoric men to be so cut and marked; on the contrary, the creation of these habits, these superstitions, these prejudices, must have taken ages. In his nature, it may be said, prehistoric man was the same as a modern savage; it is only in his acquisition that he was different.

It may be objected that if man was developed out of any kind of animal (and this is the doctrine of evolution, which, if it be not proved conclusively, has great probability and great scientific analogy in its favor) he would necessarily at first possess animal instincts; that these would only gradually be lost; that in the meantime they would serve as a protection and an aid, and that prehistoric men, therefore, would have important helps and feelings which existing savages have not. And probably of the first men, the first beings worthy to be so called, this was true: they had, or may have had, certain remnants of instincts which aided them in the struggle of existence, and as reason gradually came these instincts may have waned away. Some instincts certainly do wane when the intellect is applied steadily to their subject-matter. The curious "counting boys," the arithmetical prodigies, who can work by a strange innate faculty the most wonderful sums, lose that faculty, always partially, sometimes completely, if they are taught to reckon by rule like the rest of mankind. In like manner I have heard it said that a man could soon reason himself out of the instinct of decency if he would only take pains and work hard enough. And perhaps other primitive instincts may have in like manner passed away. But this does not affect my argument. I am only saying that these instincts, if they ever existed, *did* pass away—that there was a period, probably an immense period as we reckon time in human history, when prehistoric men lived much as savages live now, without any important aids and helps.

The proofs of this are to be found in the great works of Sir John Lubbock and Mr. Tylor, of which I just now spoke. I can only bring out two of them here. First, it is plain that the first prehistoric men had the flint tools which the lowest savages use, and we can trace a regular improvement in the finish and in the efficiency of their simple instruments corresponding to that which we see at this day in the upward transition from the lowest savages to the highest. Now, it is not conceivable that a race of beings with valuable instincts supporting their existence and supplying their wants would need these simple tools. They are exactly those needed by very poor people who have no instincts, and those were used by such, for savages are the poorest of the poor. It would be very strange if these same utensils, no more no less, were used by beings whose discerning instincts made them in comparison altogether rich. Such a being would know how to manage without such things, or if it wanted any, would know how to make better.

And, secondly, on the moral side we know that the prehistoric age was one of much licence, and the proof is that in that age descent was reckoned through the female only, just as it is among the lowest savages. "Maternity," it has been said, "is a matter of fact, paternity is a matter of opinion"; and this not very refined expression exactly conveys the connection of the lower human societies. In all slave-owning communities—in Rome formerly, and in Virginia yesterday—such was the accepted rule of law; the child kept the condition of the mother, whatever that condition was; nobody inquired as to the father; the law, once for all, assumed that he could not be ascertained. Of course no remains exist which prove this or anything else about the morality of prehistoric man; and morality can only be described by remains amounting to a history. But one of the axioms of prehistoric investigation binds us to accept this as the morality of the prehistoric races if we receive that axiom. It is plain that the widespread absence of a characteristic which greatly aids the possessor in the conflicts between race and race probably indicates that the primary race did not possess that quality. If one-armed people existed almost everywhere in every continent; if people were found in every intermediate stage, some with the mere germ of the second arm, some with the second arm halfgrown, some with it nearly complete; we should then argue "the first race cannot have had two arms, because men have always been fighting, and as two arms are a great advantage in fighting, one-armed and half-armed people would immediately have been killed off the earth; they never could have attained any numbers. A diffused deficiency in a warlike power is the best attainable evidence that the prehistoric men did not possess that power." If this axiom be received it is palpably applicable to the marriage-bond of primitive races. A cohesive "family" is the best germ for a campaigning nation. In a Roman family the boys, from the time of their birth, were bred to a domestic despotism, which well prepared them for a subjection in after life to a military discipline, a military drill, and a military despotism. They were ready to obey their generals because they were compelled to obey their fathers; they conquered the world in manhood because as children they were bred in homes where the tradition of passionate valor was steadied by the habit of implacable order. And nothing of this is possible in loosely-bound family groups (if they can be called families at all) where the father is more or less uncertain, where descent is not traced through him, where, that is, property does not come from him, where such property as he has passes to his sure relations—to his sister's children. An ill-knit nation which does not recognize paternity as a legal relation would be conquered like a mob by any other nation which had a vestige or a beginning of the *patria potestas*. If, therefore, all the first men had the strict morality of families, they would no more have permitted the rise of *semi*-moral nations anywhere in the world than the Romans would have permitted them to arise in Italy. They would have conquered, killed, and plundered them before they became nations; and yet semi-moral nations exist all over the world.

It will be said that this argument proves too much. For it proves that not only the somewhat-before-history men, but the absolutely first men, could not have had close family instincts, and yet if they were like most though not all of the animals nearest to man they had such instincts. There is a great story of some African chief who expressed his disgust at adhering to one wife by saying it was "like the monkeys." The semi-brutal ancestors of man, if they existed, had very likely an instinct of constancy which the African chief, and others like him, had lost. How, then, if it was so beneficial, could they ever lose it? The answer is plain: they could lose it if they had it as an irrational propensity and habit, and not as a moral and rational feeling. When reason came, it would weaken that habit like all other irrational habits. And reason is a force of such infinite vigor—a victory-making agent of such incomparable efficiency—that its continually diminishing valuable instincts will not matter if it grows itself steadily all the while. The strongest competitor wins in both the cases we are imagining; in the first, a race with intelligent reason, but without blind instinct, beats a race with that instinct but without that reason; in the second, a race with reason and high moral feeling beats a race with reason but without high moral feeling. And the two are palpably consistent.

There is every reason, therefore, to suppose prehistoric man to be deficient in much of sexual morality, as we regard that morality. As to the detail of "primitive marriage" or "*no* marriage," for that is pretty much what it comes to, there is of course much room for discussion. Both Mr. McLennan* and Sir John Lubbock are too accomplished reasoners and too careful investigators to wish conclusions so complex and refined as theirs to be

---

* [John Ferguson McLennan (1827–1881), Scottish sociologist, educated at Trinity College, Cambridge; influential for his research into primitive marriage customs.—*Ed.*]

accepted all in a mass, besides that on some critical points the two differ. But the main issue is not dependent on nice arguments. Upon broad grounds we may believe that in prehistoric times men fought both to gain and to keep their wives; that the strongest man took the best wife away from the weaker man; and that if the wife was restive, did not like the change, her new husband beat her; that (as in Australia now) a pretty woman was sure to undergo many such changes, and her back to bear the marks of many such chastisements; that in the principal department of human conduct (which is the most tangible and easily traced, and therefore the most obtainable specimen of the rest) the minds of prehistoric men were not so much immoral as *un*moral: they did not violate a rule of conscience, but they were somehow not sufficiently developed for them to feel on this point any conscience, or for it to prescribe to them any rule.

The same argument applies to religion. There are, indeed, many points of the greatest obscurity, both in the present savage religions and in the scanty vestiges of prehistoric religion. But one point is clear. All savage religions are full of superstitions founded on luck. Savages believe that casual omens are a sign of coming events; that some trees are lucky, that some animals are lucky, that some places are lucky, that some indifferent actions—indifferent apparently and indifferent really— are lucky, and so of others in each class, that they are unlucky. Nor can a savage well distinguish between a sign of "luck" or ill-luck, as we should say, and a deity which causes the good or the ill; the indicating precedent and the causing being are to the savage mind much the same; a steadiness of head far beyond savages is required consistently to distinguish them. And it is extremely natural that they should believe so. They are playing a game—the game of life—with no knowledge of its rules. They have not an idea of the laws of nature; if they want to cure a man, they have no conception at all of true scientific remedies. If they try anything they must try it upon bare chance. The most useful modern remedies were often discovered in this bare, empirical way. What could be more improbable—at least, for what could a prehistoric man have less given a good reason—than that some mineral springs should stop rheumatic pains, or mineral springs make wounds heal quickly? And yet the chance knowledge of the marvelous effect of gifted springs is probably as ancient as any sound knowledge as to medicine whatever. No doubt it was mere casual luck at first that tried these springs and found them answer. Somebody by accident tried them and by that accident was instantly cured. The chance which happily directed men in this one case misdirected them in a thousand cases. Some expedition had answered when the resolution to undertake it was resolved on under an ancient tree, and accordingly that tree became lucky and sacred. Another expedition failed when a magpie crossed its path, and a magpie was said to be unlucky. A serpent crossed the path of another expedition, and it had a marvelous victory, and accordingly the serpent became a sign of great luck (and what a savage cannot distinguish from it—a potent deity which makes luck). Ancient medicine is equally unreasonable: as late down as the Middle Ages it was full of superstitions founded on mere luck. The collection of prescriptions published under the direction of the Master of the Rolls abounds in such fancies, as we should call them. According to one of them, unless I forget, some disease—a fever, I think—is supposed to be cured by placing the

patient between two halves of a hare and a pigeon recently killed.* Nothing can be plainer than that there is
no ground for this kind of treatment, and that the idea
of it arose out of a chance hit, which came right and
succeeded. There was nothing so absurd or so contrary
to common sense as we are apt to imagine about it. The
lying between two halves of a hare or a pigeon was
a priori, and to the inexperienced mind, quite as likely
to cure disease as the drinking certain draughts of nas-
ty mineral water. Both, somehow, were tried; both
answered—that is, both were at the first time, or at some
memorable time, followed by a remarkable recovery; and
the only difference is that the curative power of the
mineral is persistent, and happens constantly; whereas, on
an average of trials, the proximity of a hare or pigeon is
found to have no effect, and cures take place as often in
cases where it is not tried as in cases where it is. The nature of minds which are deeply engaged in watching
events of which they do not know the reason is to single
out some fabulous accompaniment or some wonderful
series of good luck or bad luck, and to dread ever after
that accompaniment if it brings evil, and to love it and

---

* Readers of Scott's life will remember that an admirer of his
in humble life proposed to cure him of inflammation of the
bowels by making him sleep a whole night on twelve smooth
stones, painfully collected by the admirer from twelve
brooks, which was, it appeared, a *recipe* of sovereign traditional power. Scott gravely told the proposer that he had
mistaken the charm, and that the stones were of no virtue
unless wrapped up in the petticoat of a widow who never
wished to marry again, and as no such widow seems to have
been forthcoming, he escaped the remedy.

long for it if it brings good. All savages are in this position, and the fascinating effect of striking accompaniments (in some single case) of singular good fortune and singular calamity is one great source of savage religions.

Gamblers to this day are, with respect to the chance part of their game, in much the same plight as savages with respect to the main events of their whole lives. And we well know how superstitious they all are. To this day very sensible whist-players have a certain belief—not, of course, a fixed conviction, but still a certain impression—that there is "luck under a black deuce," and will half mutter some not very gentle maledictions if they turn up as a trump the four of clubs, because it brings ill-luck, and is "the devil's bedpost." Of course grown-up gamblers have too much general knowledge, too much organized common sense, to prolong or cherish such ideas; they are ashamed of entertaining them, though, nevertheless, they cannot entirely drive them out of their minds. But child-gamblers—a number of little boys set to play loo—are just in the position of savages, for their fancy is still impressible, and they have not as yet been thoroughly subjected to the confuting experience of the real world; and child gamblers have idolatries—at least I know that years ago a set of boy loo-players, of whom I was one, had considerable faith in a certain "pretty fish," which was larger and more nicely made than the other fish we had. We gave the best evidence of our belief in its power to "bring luck"; we fought for it (if our elders were out of the way); we offered to buy it with many other fish from the envied holder, and I am sure I have often cried bitterly if the chance of the game took it away from me. Persons who stand up for the dignity of philosophy, if any such there still are, will say that I ought not to mention this, because it seems trivial; but the more modest spirit of modern thought plainly teaches, if it teaches anything, the cardinal value of occasional little facts. I do not hesitate to say that many learned and elaborate explanations of the totem—the "clan" deity the beast or bird who in some supernatural way attends to the clan and watches over it—do not seem to me to be nearly as akin to the reality as it works and lives among the lower races as the "pretty fish" of my early boyhood. And very naturally so, for a grave philosopher is separated from primitive thought by the whole length of human culture; but an impressible child is as near to, and its thoughts are as much like, that thought as anything can now be.

The worst of these superstitions is that they are easy to make and hard to destroy. A single run of luck has made the fortune of many a charm and many idols. I doubt if even a single run of luck be necessary. I am sure that if an elder boy said that "the pretty fish was lucky—of course it was," all the lesser boys would believe it, and in a week it would be an accepted idol. And I suspect the Nestor of a savage tribe—the aged repository of guiding experience —would have an equal power of creating superstitions. But if once created, they are most difficult to eradicate. If anyone said that the amulet was of certain efficacy—that it always acted whenever it was applied—it would of course be very easy to disprove; but no one ever said that the "pretty fish" always brought luck; it was only said that it did so on the whole, and that if you had it you were more likely to be lucky than if you were without it. But it requires a long table of statistics of the results of games to disprove this thoroughly; and by the time people can make tables they are already above such beliefs and do not need to have them disproved. Nor in many cases where omens or amulets are used would such tables be easy to make, for the data could not be found; and a rash attempt to subdue the superstition by a striking instance may easily end in confirming it. Francis Newman,* in the remarkable narrative of his experience as a missionary in Asia, gives a curious example of this. As he was setting out on a distant and somewhat hazardous expedition, his native servants tied round the neck of the mule a small bag supposed to be of preventive and mystic virtue. As the place was crowded and a whole townspeople looking on, Mr. Newman thought that he would take an opportunity of disproving the superstition. So he made a long speech of explanation in his best Arabic, and cut off the bag, to the horror of all about him. But as ill-fortune would have it, the mule had not got thirty yards up the street before she put her foot into a hole and broke her leg; upon which all the natives were confirmed in their former faith in the power of the bag, and said: "You see now what happens to unbelievers."

Now, the present point as to these superstitions is their military inexpediency. A nation which was moved by these superstitions as to luck would be at the mercy of a nation, in other respects equal, which was not subject to them. In historical times, as we know, the panic terror at eclipses has been the ruin of the armies which have felt it;

---

* [Francis William Newman (1805–1897), brother of John Henry Newman, was a scholar, man of letters, and religious controversialist. The anecdote to which Bagehot refers is in his *Personal Narrative, in Letters: Principally from Turkey, in the Years 1830–3* (London: Holyoake), 1856, Letter LII, page 82.—Ed.]

or has made them delay to do something necessary, or rush to do something destructive. The necessity of consulting the auspices, while it was sincerely practiced and before it became a trick for disguising foresight, was in classical history very dangerous. And much worse is it with savages, whose life is one of omens, who must always consult their sorcerers, who may be turned this way or that by some chance accident, who, if they were intellectually able to frame a consistent military policy—and some savages in war see farther than in anything else—are yet liable to be put out, distracted, confused, and turned aside in the carrying out of it because some event, really innocuous but to their minds foreboding, arrests and frightens them. A religion full of omens is a military misfortune, and will bring a nation to destruction if set to fight with a nation at all equal otherwise who had a religion without omens. Clearly, then, if all early men unanimously, or even much the greater number of early men, had a religion *without* omens, no religion, or scarcely a religion, anywhere in the world could have come into existence *with* omens; the immense majority possessing the superior military advantage, the small minority destitute of it would have been crushed out and destroyed. But, on the contrary, all over the world religions with omens once existed, in most they still exist; all savages have them, and deep in the most ancient civilizations we find the plainest traces of them. Unquestionably therefore the prehistoric religion was like that of savages—*viz*, in this, that it largely consisted in the watching of omens and in the worship of lucky beasts and things, which are a sort of embodied and permanent omens.

It may indeed be objected—an analogous objection was taken as to the ascertained moral deficiencies of prehistoric mankind—that if this religion of omens was so pernicious and so likely to ruin a race, no race would ever have acquired it. But it is only likely to ruin a race contending with another race otherwise equal. The fancied discovery of these omens—not an extravagant thing in an early age, as I have tried to show, not a whit then to be distinguished as improbable from the discovery of healing herbs or springs which prehistoric men also did discover—the discovery of omens was an act of reason as far as it went. And if in reason the omen-finding race were superior to the races in conflict with them, the omen-finding race would win, and we may conjecture that omen-finding races were thus superior since they won and prevailed in every latitude and in every zone.

In all particulars therefore we would keep to our formula and say that prehistoric man was substantially a savage like present savages, in morals, intellectual attainments, and in religion; but that he differed in this from our present savages, that he had not had time to ingrain his nature so deeply with bad habits, and to impress bad beliefs so unalterably on his mind as they have. They have had ages to fix the stain on themselves, but primitive man was younger and had no such time.

I have elaborated the evidence for this conclusion at what may seem needless and tedious length, but I have done so on account of its importance. If we accept it, and if we are sure of it, it will help us to many most important conclusions. Some of these I have dwelt upon in previous papers, but I will set them down again.

First, it will in part explain to us what the world was about, so to speak, before history. It was making, so to say, the intellectual *consistence*—the connected and coherent habits, the preference of equable to violent enjoyment, the abiding capacity to prefer, if required, the future to the present, the mental prerequisites without which civilization could not begin to exist, and without which it would soon cease to exist even had it begun. The primitive man, like the present savage, had not these prerequisites, but, unlike the present savage, he was capable of acquiring them and of being trained in them, for his nature was still soft and still impressible, and possibly, strange as it may seem to say, his outward circumstances were more favorable to an attainment of civilization than those of our present savages. At any rate, the prehistoric times were spent in making men capable of writing a history, and having something to put in it when it is written, and we can see how it was done.

Two preliminary processes indeed there are which seem inscrutable. There was some strange preliminary process by which the main races of men were formed; they began to exist very early, and except by intermixture no new ones have been formed since. It was a process singularly active in early ages, and singularly quiescent in later ages. Such differences as exist between the Aryan, the Turanian, the Negro, the red man, and the Australian are differences greater altogether than any causes now active are capable of creating in present men, at least in any way explicable by us. And there is, therefore, a strong presumption that (as great authorities now hold) these differences were created before the nature of men, especially before the mind and the adaptive nature of men, had taken their existing constitution. And a second condition precedent of civilization seems, at least to me, to have been equally inherited, if the doctrine of evolution be true, from some previous state or condition. I at least find it difficult to conceive of men, at all like the present men, unless existing in something like families; that is, in groups avowedly connected, at least on the mother's side, and probably always with a vestige of connection, more or less, on the father's side, and unless these groups were like many animals, gregarious, under a leader more or less fixed. It is almost beyond imagination how man, as we know man, could by any sort of process have gained this step in civilization. And it is a great advantage, to say the least of it, in the evolution theory that it enables us to remit this difficulty to a pre-existing period in nature, where other instincts and powers than our present ones may perhaps have come into play, and where our imagination can hardly travel. At any rate, for the present I may assume these two steps in human progress made, and these two conditions realized.

The rest of the way, if we grant these two conditions, is plainer. The first thing is the erection of what we may call a custom-making power; that is, of an authority which can enforce a fixed rule of life, which, by means of that fixed rule, can in some degree create a calculable future, which can make it rational to postpone present violent but momentary pleasure for future continual pleasure, because it ensures, what else is not sure, that if the sacrifice of what is in hand be made, enjoyment of the contingent expected recompense will be received. Of course I am not saying that we shall find in early society any authority of which these shall be the motives. We must have traveled ages (unless all our evidence be wrong) from the first men before there was a comprehension of such motives. I only mean that the first thing in early society was an authority of whose action this shall be the result, little as it knew what it was doing, little as it would have cared if it had known.

Nation-making (continued)

The conscious end of early societies was not at all, or scarcely at all, the protection of life and property, as it was assumed to be by the eighteenth-century theory of government. Even in early historical ages—in the youth of the human race, not its childhood—such is not the nature of early states. Sir Henry Maine has taught us that the earliest subject of jurisprudence is not the separate property of the individual, but the common property of the family group; what we should call private property hardly then existed; or if it did, was so small as to be of no importance: it was like the things little children are now allowed to *call* their own, which they feel it very hard to have taken from them, but which they have no real right to hold and keep. Such is our earliest property-law, and our earliest life-law is that the lives of all members of the family group were at the mercy of the head of the group. As far as the individual goes, neither his goods nor his existence were protected at all. And this may teach us that something else was lacked in early societies besides what in our societies we now think of.

I do not think I put this too high when I say that a most important if not the most important object of early legislation was the enforcement of lucky rites. I do not like to say religious rites, because that would involve me in a great controversy as to the power, or even the existence, of early religions. But there is no savage tribe without a notion of luck; and perhaps there is hardly any which has not a conception of luck for the tribe as a tribe, of which each member has not some such a belief that his own action or the action of any other member of it—that he or the others doing anything which was unluckier would bring a "curse"—might cause evil not only to himself, but to all the tribe as well. I have said so much about "luck" and about its naturalness before, that I ought to say nothing again. But I must add that the contagiousness of the idea of "luck" is remarkable. It does not at all, like the notion of desert, cleave to the doer. There are people to this day who would not permit in their house people to sit down thirteen to dinner. They do not expect any evil to themselves particularly for permitting it or sharing in it, but they cannot get out of their heads the idea that some one or more of the number will come to harm if the thing is done. This is what Mr. Tylor calls survival in culture. The faint belief in the corporate liability of these thirteen is the feeble relic and last dying representative of that great principle of corporate liability to good and ill fortune which has filled such an immense place in the world.

The traces of it are endless. You can hardly take up a book of travels in rude regions without finding "I wanted to do so and so. But I was not permitted, for the natives feared it might bring ill luck on the 'party,' or perhaps the tribe." Mr. Galton,* for instance, could hardly feed his people. The Damaras, he says, have numberless superstitions about meat which are very troublesome. In the first place, each tribe, or rather family, is prohibited from eating cattle of certain colors, savages "who come from the sun" eschewing sheep spotted in a particular way, which those "who come from the rain" have no objection to. "As," he says, "there are five or six eandas or descents, and I had men from most of them with me, I could hardly kill a sheep that everybody would eat"; and he

---

* [*The Narrative of an Explorer in Tropical South Africa*, by Francis Galton (London: John Murray, 1853), pages 137–138.—Ed.]

could not keep his meat, for it had to be given away because it was commanded by one superstition, nor buy
milk, the staple food of those parts, because it was
prohibited by another. And so on without end. Doing
anything unlucky is in their idea what putting on something that attracts the electric fluid is in fact. You cannot
be sure that harm will not be done, not only to the person
in fault, but to those about him too. As in the Scriptural
phrase, doing what is of evil omen is "like one that letteth
out water." He cannot tell what are the consequences of
his act, who will share them, or how they can be
prevented.

In the earliest historical nations I need not say that the
corporate liabilities of states is to a modern student their
most curious feature. The belief is indeed raised far above
the notion of mere "luck," because there is a distinct
belief in gods or a god whom the act offends. But the in-
discriminate character of the punishment still survives;
not only the mutilator of the Hermae, but all the Athenians—not only the violator of the rites of the *Bona dea*,
but all the Romans—are liable to the curse engendered;
and so all through ancient history. The strength of the
corporate anxiety so created is known to everyone. Not
only was it greater than any anxiety about personal
property, but it was immeasurably greater. Naturally,
even reasonably we may say, it was greater. The dread of
the powers of nature, or of the beings who rule those
powers, is properly, upon grounds of reason, as much
greater than any other dread as the might of the powers
of nature is superior to that of any other powers. If a
tribe or a nation have, by a contagious fancy, come to
believe that the doing of any one thing by any number
will be "unlucky"—that is, will bring an intense and vast

liability on them all—then that tribe and that nation will prevent the doing of that thing more than anything else. They will deal with the most cherished chief who even by chance should do it as in a similar case the sailors dealt with Jonah.

I do not of course mean that this strange condition of mind as it seems to us was the sole source of early customs. On the contrary, man might be described as a custom-making animal with more justice than by many of the short descriptions. In whatever way a man has done anything once, he has a tendency to do it again: if he has done it several times he has a great tendency so to do it, and what is more, he has a great tendency to make others do it also. He transmits his formed customs to his children by example and by teaching. This is true now of human nature, and will always be true, no doubt. But what is peculiar in early societies is that over most of these customs there grows sooner or later a semi-supernatural sanction. The whole community is possessed with the idea that if the primal usages of the tribe be broken, harm unspeakable will happen in ways you cannot think of, and from sources you cannot imagine. As people nowadays believe that "murder will out," and that great crime will bring even an earthly punishment, so in early times people believed that for any breach of sacred custom certain retribution would happen. To this day many semi-civilized races have great difficulty in regarding any arrangement as binding and conclusive unless they can also manage to look at it, as an inherited usage. Sir H. Maine, in his last work, gives a most curious case. The English Government in India has in many cases made new and great works of irrigation, of which no ancient Indian government ever thought; and it has generally left it to the native village community to say what share each man of the village should have in the water; and the village authorities have accordingly laid down a series of most minute rules about it. But the peculiarity is that in no case do these rules "purport to emanate from the personal authority of their author or authors (which rests on grounds of reason not on grounds of innocence and sanctity), nor do they assume to be dictated by a sense of equity; there is always, I am assured, a sort of fiction under which some customs as to the distribution of water are supposed to have emanated from a remote antiquity, although, in fact, no such artificial supply had ever been so much as thought of."* So difficult does this ancient race—like, probably, in this respect so much of the ancient world—find it to imagine a rule which is obligatory, but not traditional.

The ready formation of custom-making groups in early society must have been greatly helped by the easy divisions of that society. Much of the world—all Europe, for example—was then covered by the primeval forest; men had only conquered, and as yet could only conquer, a few plots and corners from it. These narrow spaces were soon exhausted, and if numbers grew, some of the new people must move. Accordingly, migrations were constant, and were necessary. And these migrations were not like those of modern times. There was no such feeling as binds, even Americans who hate, or speak as if they hated, the present political England—nevertheless to "the old

---

* [Lecture IV, "The Eastern Village Community," from *Village Communities in the East and West: Six Lectures Delivered at Oxford*, by Henry Sumner Maine (London: John Murray, 1871), pages 109–110.—*Ed.*]

home." There was then no organized means of communication—no practical communication, we may say,
between parted members of the same group; those who
once went out from the parent society went out for ever;
they left no abiding remembrance, and they kept no
abiding regard. Even the language of the parent tribe and
of the descended tribe would differ in a generation or
two. There being no written literature and no spoken intercourse, the speech of both would vary (the speech of
such communities is always varying), and would vary in
different directions. One set of causes, events, and associations would act on one, and another set on another;
sectional differences would soon arise, and, for speaking
purposes, what philologists call a dialectical difference
often amounts to real and total difference: no connected
interchange of thought is possible any longer. Separate
groups soon "set up house"; the early societies begin a
new set of customs, acquire and keep a distinct and special "luck."

If it were not for this facility of new formations, one
good or bad custom would long since have "corrupted"
the world; but even this would not have been enough but
for those continual wars of which I have spoken at such
length in the essay on "The Use of Conflict" that I need
say nothing now. These are by their incessant fractures of
old images, and by their constant infusion of new elements, the real regenerators of society. And whatever be
the truth or falsehood of the general dislike to mixed and
half-bred races, no such suspicion was probably applicable to the early mixtures of primitive society. Supposing, as is likely, each great aboriginal race to have had its
own quarter of the world (a quarter, as it would seem,
corresponding to the special quarters in which plants and

animals are divided), then the immense majority of the mixtures would be between men of different tribes but of the same stock, and this no one would object to, but everyone would praise.

In general, too, the conquerors would be better than the conquered (most merits in early society are more or less military merits), but they would not be very much better, for the lowest steps in the ladder of civilization are very steep, and the effort to mount them is slow and tedious. And this is probably the better if they are to produce a good and quick effect in civilizing those they have conquered. The experience of the English in India shows—if it shows anything—that a highly civilized race may fail in producing a rapidly excellent effect on a less civilized race, because it is too good and too different. The two are not *en rapport* together; the merits of the one are not the merits prized by the other; the manner-language of the one is not the manner-language of the other. The higher being is not and cannot be a model for the lower; he could not mold himself on it if he would, and would not if he could. Consequently, the two races have long lived together, "near and yet far off," daily seeing one another and daily interchanging superficial thoughts, but in the depths of their mind separated by a whole era of civilization, and so affecting one another only a little in comparison with what might have been hoped. But in early societies there were no such great differences, and the rather superior conqueror must have easily improved the rather inferior conquered.

It is in the interior of these customary groups that national characters are formed. As I wrote a whole essay on the manner of this before, I cannot speak of it now. By proscribing nonconformist members for generations, and

cherishing and rewarding conformist members, nonconformists become fewer and fewer, and conformists more
and more. Most men mostly imitate what they see, and
catch the tone of what they hear, and so a settled type—
a persistent character—is formed. Nor is the process
wholly mental. I cannot agree, though the greatest authorities say it, that no "unconscious selection" has been
at work at the breed of man. If neither that nor conscious
selection has been at work, how did there come to be
these breeds, and such there are in the greatest numbers,
though we call them nations? In societies tyrannically
customary, uncongenial minds become first cowed, then
melancholy, then out of health, and at last die. A Shelley
in New England could hardly have lived, and a race of
Shelleys would have been impossible. Mr. Galton wishes
that breeds of men should be created by matching men
with marked characteristics with women of like characteristics. But surely this is what nature has been doing
time out of mind, and most in the rudest nations and
hardest times. Nature disheartened in each generation the
ill-fitted members of each customary group, so deprived
them of their full vigor, or, if they were weakly, killed
them. The Spartan character was formed because none
but people with a Spartan make of mind could endure a
Spartan existence. The early Roman character was so
formed too. Perhaps all very marked national characters
can be traced back to a time of rigid and pervading discipline. In modern times, when society is more tolerant,
new national characters are neither so strong, so featurely, nor so uniform.

In this manner society was occupied in prehistoric
times—it is consistent with and explicable by our general
principle as to savages that society should for ages have

been so occupied, strange as that conclusion is, and incredible as it would be if we had not been taught by experience to believe strange things.

Secondly, this principle and this conception of prehistoric times explain to us the meaning and the origin of the oldest and strangest of social anomalies—an anomaly which is among the first things history tells us—the existence of *caste* nations. Nothing is at first sight stranger than the aspect of those communities where several nations seem to be bound up together—where each is governed by its own rule of law, where no one pays any deference to the rule of law of any of the others. But if our principles be true, these are just the nations most likely to last, which would have a special advantage in early times, and would probably not only maintain themselves, but conquer and kill out others also. The characteristic necessity of early society, as we have seen, is strict usage and binding coercive custom. But the obvious result and inevitable evil of that is monotony in society; no one can be much different from his fellows, or can cultivate his difference.

Such societies are necessarily weak from the want of variety in their elements. But a *caste* nation is various and composite; and has in a mode suited to early societies the constant co-operation of contrasted persons, which in a later age is one of the greatest triumphs of civilization. In a primitive age the division between the warrior caste and the priestly caste is especially advantageous. Little popular and little deserving to be popular nowadays as are priestly hierarchies, most probably the beginnings of science were made in such, and were for ages transmitted in such. An intellectual class was in that age only possible when it was protected by a notion that whoever hurt

them would certainly be punished by heaven. In this class
apart discoveries were slowly made and some beginning
of mental discipline was slowly matured. But such a
community is necessarily unwarlike, and the superstition
which protects priests from home murder will not aid
them in conflict with the foreigner. Few nations mind
killing their enemies' priests, and many priestly civilizations have perished without record before they well
began. But such a civilization will not perish if a warrior
caste is tacked on to it and is bound to defend it. On
the contrary, such a civilization will be singularly likely
to live. The head of the sage will help the arm of the
soldier.

That a nation divided into *castes* must be a most difficult thing to found is plain. Probably it could only begin
in a country several times conquered, and where the
boundaries of each *caste* rudely coincided with the boundaries of certain sets of victors and vanquished. But, as
we now see, when founded it is a likely nation to last. A
parti-colored community of many tribes and many usages
is more likely to get on, and help itself, than a nation of a
single lineage and one monotonous rule. I say "at first,"
because I apprehend that in this case, as in so many
others in the puzzling history of progress, the very institutions which most aid at step number one are precisely
those which most impede at step number two. The whole
of a caste nation is more various than the whole of a
non-caste nation, but each caste itself is more monotonous than anything is, or can be, in a non-caste nation.
Gradually a habit of action and type of mind forces itself
on each caste, and it is little likely to be rid of it, for all
who enter it are taught in one way and trained to the
same employment. Several non-caste nations have still

continued to progress. But all caste nations have stopped early, though some have lasted long. Each color in the singular composite of these tessellated societies has an indelible and invariable shade.

Thirdly, we see why so few nations have made rapid advance, and how many have become stationary. It is in the process of becoming a nation, and in order to become such, that they subjected themselves to the influence which has made them stationary. They could not become a real nation without binding themselves by a fixed law and usage, and it is the fixity of that law and usage which has kept them as they were ever since. I wrote a whole essay on this before, so I need say nothing now; and I only name it because it is one of the most important consequences of this view of society, if not indeed the most important.

Again, we can thus explain one of the most curious facts of the present world. "Manner," says a shrewd observer, who has seen much of existing life, "manner gets regularly worse as you go from the East to the West; it is best in Asia, not so good in Europe, and altogether bad in the western states of America." And the reason is this—an imposing manner is a dignified usage, which tends to preserve itself and also all other existing usages along with itself. It tends to induce the obedience of mankind. One of the cleverest novelists of the present day has a curious dissertation to settle why on the hunting field, and in all collections of men, some men "snub and some men get snubbed"; and why society recognizes in each case the ascendancy or the subordination as if it was right. "It is not at all," Mr. Trollope* fully explains, "rare

* [Anthony Trollope (1815–1882), English novelist. I have not

133

ability which gains the supremacy; very often the ill-treated man is quite as clever as the man who ill-treats him. Nor does it absolutely depend on wealth; for, though great wealth is almost always a protection from social ignominy, and will always ensure a passive respect, it will not in a miscellaneous group of men of itself gain an active power to snub others. Schoolboys, in the same way," the novelist adds, "let some boys have dominion, and make other boys slaves." And he decides, no doubt truly, that in each case "something in the manner or gait" of the supreme boy or man has much to do with it. On this account in early society a dignified manner is of essential importance; it is, then, not only an auxiliary mode of acquiring respect, but a principal mode. The competing institutions which have now much superseded it had not then begun. Ancient institutions or venerated laws did not then exist; and the habitual ascendancy of grave manner was a primary force in winning and calming mankind. To this day it is rare to find a savage chief without it; and almost always they greatly excel in it. Only last year a red Indian chief came from the prairies to see President Grant, and everybody declared that he had the best manners in Washington. The secretaries and heads of departments seemed vulgar to him; though, of course, intrinsically they were infinitely above him, for he was only "a plundering rascal." But an impressive manner had been a tradition in the societies in which he had lived, be-

---

been able to trace this passage exactly as Bagehot gives it; there are many such hunting scenes in Trollope, however. One very similar to what Bagehot quotes occurs in *Can You Forgive Her?* (1866), Chapter 16.—*Ed.*]

cause it was of great value in those societies; and it is not a tradition in America, for nowhere is it less thought of, or of less use, than in a rough English colony; the essentials of civilization there depend on far different influences.

And manner being so useful and so important, usages and customs grow up to develop it. Asiatic society is full of such things, if it should not rather be said to be composed of them.

"From the spirit and decision of a public envoy upon ceremonies and forms," says Sir John Malcolm,

the Persians very generally form their opinion of the character of the country he represents. This fact I had read in books, and all I saw convinced me of its truth. Fortunately the Elchee had resided at some of the principal courts of India, whose usages are very similar. He was, therefore, deeply versed in that important science denominated "Kâida-e-nishest-oo-berkhâst" (or the art of sitting and rising), in which is included a knowledge of the forms and manners of good society, and particularly those of Asiatic kings and their courts.

He was quite aware, on his first arrival in Persia, of the consequence of every step he took on such delicate points; he was, therefore, anxious to fight all his battles regarding ceremonies before he came near the footstool of royalty. We were consequently plagued, from the moment we landed at Abusheher, till we reached Shiraz, with daily almost hourly drilling that we might be perfect in our demeanor at all places, and under all circumstances. We were carefully instructed where to ride in a procession, where to stand or sit within-doors, when to rise from our seats, how far to advance to meet a visitor, and to what part of the tent or house we were to follow him when he departed, if he was of sufficient rank to make us stir a step.

The regulations of our risings and standings, and movings and reseatings, were, however, of comparatively less importance than the time and manner of smoking our Kelliâns and taking our coffee. It is quite astonishing how much depends upon coffee and tobacco in Persia. Men are gratified or offended, according to the mode in which these favorite refreshments are offered. You welcome a visitor, or send him off, by the way in which you call for a pipe or a cup of coffee. Then you mark, in the most minute manner, every shade of attention and consideration, by the mode in which he is treated. If he be above you, you present these refreshments yourself, and do not partake till commanded; if equal, you exchange pipes, and present him with coffee, taking the next cup yourself; if a little below you, and you wish to pay him attention, you leave him to smoke his own pipe, but the servant gives him, according to your condescending nod, the first cup of coffee; if much inferior, you keep your distance and maintain your rank, by taking the first cup of coffee yourself, and then directing the servant, by a wave of the hand, to help the guest.

When a visitor arrives, the coffee and pipe are called for to welcome him; a second call for these articles announces that he may depart; but this part of the ceremony varies according to the relative rank or intimacy of the parties.

These matters may appear light to those with whom observances of this character are habits, not rules; but in this country they are of primary consideration, a

man's importance with himself and with others de-
pending on them.*

In ancient customary societies the influence of manner,
which is a primary influence, has been settled into rules,
so that it may aid established usages and not thwart
them—that it may, above all, augment the *habit* of going
by custom, and not break and weaken it. Every aid, as we
have seen, was wanted to impose the yoke of custom
upon such societies; and impressing the power of manner
to serve them was one of the greatest aids.

And lastly, we now understand why order and civilization are so unstable even in progressive communities. We
see frequently in states what physiologists call "atavism"
—the return, in part, to the unstable nature of their barbarous ancestors. Such scenes of cruelty and horror as
happened in the great French Revolution, and as happen,
more or less, in every great riot, have always been said to
bring out a secret and suppressed side of human nature;
and we now see that they were the outbreak of inherited
passions long repressed by fixed custom, but starting into
life as soon as that repression was catastrophically removed, and when sudden choice was given. The irrita-
bility of mankind, too, is only part of their imperfect,
transitory civilization and of their original savage nature.
They could not look steadily to a given end for an hour in
their prehistoric state; and even now, when excited or
when suddenly and wholly thrown out of their old

* [Sir John Malcolm (1805–1893), Anglo-Indian administrator
  and travel writer. This passage is from volume I of *Sketches
  of Persia: From the Journals of a Traveller in the East* (London: John Murray, 1827), pages 119–120.—*Ed.*]

grooves, they can scarcely do so. Even some very high races, as the French and the Irish, seem in troubled times hardly to be stable at all, but to be carried everywhere as the passions of the moment and the ideas generated at the hour may determine. But, thoroughly to deal with such phenomena as these, we must examine the mode in which national characters can be emancipated from the rule of custom, and can be prepared for the use of choice.

5

The Age of Discussion

T HE GREATEST living contrast is between the old Eastern and customary civilizations and the new Western
and changeable civilizations. A year or two ago an inquiry was made of our most intelligent officers in the
East, not as to whether the English Government were
really doing good in the East, but as to whether the natives of India themselves thought we were doing good;
to which, in a majority of cases, the officers who were the
best authority answered thus: "No doubt you are giving
the Indians many great benefits: you give them continued
peace, free trade, the right to live as they like, subject
to the laws; in these points and others they are far better
off than they ever were; but still they cannot make you
out. What puzzles them is your constant disposition to
change, or as you call it, improvement. Their own life in
every detail being regulated by ancient usage, they cannot
comprehend a policy which is always bringing something
new; they do not a bit believe that the desire to make
them comfortable and happy is the root of it; they
believe, on the contrary, that you are aiming at something
which they do not understand—that you mean to 'take

away their religion'; in a word, that the end and object of all these continual changes is to make Indians not what they are and what they like to be, but something new and different from what they are, and what they would not like to be." In the East, in a word, we are attempting to put new wine into old bottles—to pour what we can of a civilization whose spirit is progress into the form of a civilization whose spirit is fixity, and whether we shall succeed or not is perhaps the most interesting question in an age abounding almost beyond example in questions of political interest.

Historical inquiries show that the feeling of the Hindoos is the old feeling, and that the feeling of the Englishman is a modern feeling. "Old law rests," as Sir Henry Maine puts it, "not on contract but on status."* The life of ancient civilization, so far as legal records go, runs back to a time when every important particular of life was settled by a usage which was social, political, and religious, as we should now say, all in one—which those who obeyed it could not have been able to analyze, for those distinctions had no place in their mind and language, but which they felt to be a usage of imperishable import, and above all things to be kept unchanged. In former papers I have shown, or at least tried to show, why these customary civilizations were the only ones which suited an early society; why, so to say, they alone could have been first; in what manner they had in their very structure a decisive advantage over all competitors. But now comes the further question: If fixity is an invariable ingredient in early civilizations, how then did any civilization become unfixed? No doubt most civilizations

* [*Ancient Law*, page 164.—*Ed.*]

stuck where they first were; no doubt we see now why
stagnation is the rule of the world, and why progress is
the very rare exception; but we do not learn what it is
which has caused progress in these few cases, or the absence of what it is which has denied it in all others. To
this question history gives a very clear and very remarkable answer. It is that the change from the age of status to
the age of choice was first made in states where the
government was to a great and a growing extent a
government by discussion, and where the subjects of that
discussion were in some degree abstract, or, as we should
say, matters of principle. It was in the small republics of
Greece and Italy that the chain of custom was first
broken. "Liberty said, Let there be light, and, like a sunrise on the sea, Athens arose," says Shelley,* and his historical philosophy is in this case far more correct than is
usual with him. A free state—a state with liberty—means
a state, call it republic or call it monarchy, in which the
sovereign power is divided between many persons, and in
which there is a discussion among those persons. Of these
the Greek republics were the first in history, if not in time,
and Athens was the greatest of those republics.

After the event it is easy to see why the teaching of history should be this and nothing else. It is easy to see why
the common discussion of common actions or common
interests should become the root of change and progress.
In early society, originality in life was forbidden and
repressed by the fixed rule of life. It may not have been

* [St. John-Stevas points out that the actual lines from Shelley
are: "Let there be light! said Liberty; / And like sunrise from
the sea, / Athens arose!" *Hellas: A Lyrical Drama*, lines
682–684.—Ed.]

quite so much so in ancient Greece as in some other parts of the world. But it was very much so even there. As a recent writer has well said, "Law then presented itself to men's minds as something venerable and unchangeable, as old as the city; it had been delivered by the founder himself, when he laid the walls of the city, and kindled its sacred fire." An ordinary man who wished to strike out a new path, to begin a new and important practice by himself, would have been peremptorily required to abandon his novelties on pain of death; he was deviating, he would be told, from the ordinances imposed by the gods on his nation, and he must not do so to please himself. On the contrary, others were deeply interested in his actions. If he disobeyed, the gods might inflict grievous harm on all the people as well as him. Each partner in the most ancient kind of partnerships was supposed to have the power of attracting the wrath of the divinities on the entire firm, upon the other partners quite as much as upon himself. The quaking bystanders in a superstitious age would soon have slain an isolated bold man in the beginning of his innovations. What Macaulay so relied on as the incessant source of progress—the desire of man to better his condition—was not then permitted to work; man was required to live as his ancestors had lived.

Still further away from those times were the "free thought" and the "advancing sciences" of which we now hear so much. The first and most natural subject upon which human thought concerns itself is religion; the first wish of the half-emancipated thinker is to use his reason on the great problems of human destiny—to find out whence he came and whither he goes, to form for himself the most reasonable idea of God which he can form. But, as Mr. Grote happily said—"This is usually what ancient times would not let a man do. His *gens* or his φρατρία required him to believe as they believed."* Toleration is of all ideas the most modern, because the notion that the bad religion of A cannot impair, here or hereafter, the welfare of B is, strange to say, a modern idea. And the help of "science," at that stage of thought, is still more nugatory. Physical science, as we conceive it—that is, the systematic investigation of external nature in detail—did not then exist. A few isolated observations on surface things—a half-correct calendar, secrets mainly of priestly invention, and in priestly custody—were all that was then imagined; the idea of using a settled study of nature as a basis for the discovery of new instruments and new things did not then exist. It is indeed a modern idea, and is peculiar to a few European countries even yet. In the most intellectual city of the ancient world, in its most intellectual age, Socrates, its most intellectual inhabitant, discouraged the study of physics because it engendered uncertainty, and did not augment human happiness. The kind of knowledge which is most connected with human progress now was that least connected with it then.

But a government by discussion, if it can be borne, at once breaks down the yoke of fixed custom. The idea of the two is inconsistent. As far as it goes, the mere putting up of a subject to discussion, with the object of being guided by that discussion, is a clear admission that that subject is in no degree settled by established rule, and that men are free to choose in it. It is an admission too that there is no sacred authority—no one transcendent and

---

* [I have not been able to trace this quotation. But Grote discusses these clan and kinship relations in Volume 3, Chapter 10 of his *History of Greece* (1846–1856).—*Ed.*]

divinely appointed man whom in that matter the community is bound to obey. And if a single subject or group of subjects be once admitted to discussion, ere long the habit of discussion comes to be established, the sacred charm of use and wont to be dissolved. "Democracy," it has been said in modern times, "is like the grave; it takes, but it does not give." The same is true of "discussion." Once effectually submit a subject to that ordeal and you can never withdraw it again; you can never again clothe it with mystery, or fence it by consecration; it remains for ever open to free choice, and exposed to profane deliberation.

The only subjects which can be first submitted, or which till a very late age of civilization can be submitted to discussion in the community, are the questions involving the visible and pressing interests of the community; they are political questions of high and urgent import. If a nation has in any considerable degree gained the habit, and exhibited the capacity, to discuss these questions with freedom, and to decide them with discretion, to argue much on politics and not to argue ruinously, an enormous advance in other kinds of civilization may confidently be predicted for it. And the reason is a plain deduction from the principles which we have found to guide early civilization. The first prehistoric men were passionate savages, with the greatest difficulty coerced into order and compressed into a state. For ages were spent in beginning that order and founding that state; the only sufficient and effectual agent in so doing was consecrated custom; but then that custom gathered over everything, arrested all onward progress, and stayed the originality of mankind. If, therefore, a nation is able to gain the benefit of custom without the evil—if after ages of waiting it can have order and choice together—at once the fatal clog is removed, and the ordinary springs of progress, as in a modern community we conceive them, begin their elastic action.

Discussion, too, has incentives to progress peculiar to itself. It gives a premium to intelligence. To set out the arguments required to determine political action with such force and effect that they really should determine it, is a high and great exertion of intellect. Of course, all such arguments are produced under conditions; the argument abstractedly best is not necessarily the winning argument. Political discussion must move those who have to act; it must be framed in the ideas, and be consonant with the precedent, of its time, just as it must speak its language. But within these marked conditions good discussion is better than bad; no people can bear a government of discussion for a day which does not, within the boundaries of its prejudices and its ideas, prefer good reasoning to bad reasoning, sound argument to unsound. A prize for argumentative mind is given in free states, to which no other states have anything to compare.

Tolerance too is learned in discussion, and, as history shows, is only so learned. In all customary societies bigotry is the ruling principle. In rude places to this day anyone who says anything new is looked on with suspicion, and is persecuted by opinion if not injured by penalty. One of the greatest pains to human nature is the pain of a new idea. It is, as common people say, so "upsetting"; it makes you think that, after all, your favorite notions may be wrong, your firmest beliefs ill-founded; it is certain that till now there was no place allotted in your mind to the new and startling inhabitant, and now that it has conquered an entrance, you do not at once see which of your old ideas it will or will not turn out, with which of them it can be reconciled, and with which it is at essential enmity. Naturally, therefore, common men hate a new idea, and are disposed more or less to ill-treat the original man who brings it. Even nations with long habits of discussion are intolerant enough. In England, where there is on the whole probably a freer discussion of a greater number of subjects than ever was before in the world, we know how much power bigotry retains. But discussion, to be successful, requires tolerance. It fails wherever, as in a French political assembly, anyone who hears anything which he dislikes tries to howl it down. If we know that a nation is capable of enduring continuous discussion, we know that it is capable of practicing with equanimity continuous tolerance.

The power of a government by discussion as an instrument of elevation plainly depends—other things being equal—on the greatness or littleness of the things to be discussed. There are periods when great ideas are "in the air," and when, from some cause or other, even common persons seem to partake of an unusual elevation. The age of Elizabeth in England was conspicuously such a time. The new idea of the Reformation in religion, and the enlargement of the *moenia mundi** by the discovery of new and singular lands, taken together, gave an impulse to thought which few, if any, ages can equal. The discussion, though not wholly free, was yet far freer than in the average of ages and countries. Accordingly, every pursuit seemed to start forward. Poetry, science, and architecture, different as they are, and removed as they all are at first sight from such an influence as discussion, were suddenly

---

* [*Moenia mundi*: the walls or limits of the world. The phrase is from Lucretius, *De rerum natura*, I:73.—*Ed.*]

started onward. Macaulay would have said you might rightly read the power of discussion "in the poetry of Shakespeare, in the prose of Bacon, in the oriels of Longleat, and the stately pinnacles of Burleigh." This is, in truth, but another case of the principle of which I have had occasion to say so much as to the character of ages and countries. If any particular power is much prized in an age, those possessed of that power will be imitated; those deficient in that power will be despised. In consequence an unusual quantity of that power will be developed, and be conspicuous. Within certain limits vigorous and elevated thought was respected in Elizabeth's time, and, therefore, vigorous and elevated thinkers were many; and the effect went far beyond the cause. It penetrated into physical science, for which very few men cared; and it began a reform in philosophy to which almost all were then opposed. In a word, the temper of the age encouraged originality, and in consequence original men started into prominence, went hither and thither where they liked, arrived at goals which the age never expected, and so made it ever memorable.

In this manner all the great movements of thought in ancient and modern times have been nearly connected in time with government by discussion. Athens, Rome, the Italian republics of the Middle Ages, the *communes* and states-general of feudal Europe, have all had a special and peculiar quickening influence, which they owed to their freedom, and which states without that freedom have never communicated. And it has been at the time of great epochs of thought—at the Peloponnesian War, at the fall of the Roman Republic, at the Reformation, at the French Revolution—that such liberty of speaking and thinking have produced their full effect.

It is on this account that the discussions of savage tribes have produced so little effect in emancipating those tribes from their despotic customs. The oratory of the North American Indian—the first savage whose peculiarities fixed themselves in the public imagination—has become celebrated, and yet the North American Indians were scarcely, if at all, better orators than many other savages. Almost all of the savages who have melted away before the Englishman were better speakers than he is. But the oratory of the savages has led to nothing, and was likely to lead to nothing. It is a discussion not of principles, but of undertakings; its topics are whether expedition A will answer, and should be undertaken; whether expedition B will not answer, and should not be undertaken; whether village A is the best village to plunder, or whether village B is a better. Such discussions augment the vigor of language, encourage a debating facility, and develop those gifts of demeanor and of gesture which excite the confidence of the hearers. But they do not excite the speculative intellect, do not lead men to argue speculative doctrines, or to question ancient principles. They, in some material respects, improve the sheep within the fold; but they do not help them or incline them to leap out of the fold.

The next question, therefore, is: Why did discussions in some cases relate to prolific ideas, and why did discussions in other cases relate only to isolated transactions? The reply which history suggests is very clear and very remarkable. Some races of men at our earliest knowledge of them have already acquired the basis of a free constitution; they have already the rudiments of a complex polity—a monarch, a senate, and a general meeting of citizens. The Greeks were one of those races, and it happened, as was natural, that there was in process of time a struggle, the earliest that we know of, between the aristocratical party, originally represented by the senate, and the popular party, represented by the "general meeting." This is plainly a question of principle, and its being so has led to its history being written more than two thousand years afterwards in a very remarkable manner. Some seventy years ago an English country gentleman named Mitford,* who, like so many of his age, had been terrified into aristocratic opinions by the first French Revolution, suddenly found that the history of the Peloponnesian War was the reflex of his own time. He took up his Thucydides, and there he saw, as in a mirror, the progress and the struggles of his age. It required some freshness of mind to see this; at least, it had been hidden for many centuries. All the modern histories of Greece before Mitford had but the vaguest idea of it; and not being a man of supreme originality, he would doubtless have had very little idea of it either, except that the analogy of what he saw helped him by a telling object-lesson to the understanding of what he read. Just as in every country of Europe in 1793 there were two factions, one of the old-world aristocracy, and the other of the incoming democracy, just so there was in every city of ancient Greece, in the year 400 B.C., one party of the many and another of the few. This Mr. Mitford perceived, and being a strong aristocrat, he wrote a "history," which is little except a party pamphlet, and which, it must be said, is even now readable on that very account. The vigor of passion with which it was

* [William Mitford (1744–1827), Tory historian, officer, member of Parliament. His multi-volume *History of Greece* was published in 1795.—*Ed.*]

written puts life into the words, and retains the attention of the reader. And that is not all. Mr. Grote, the great scholar whom we have had lately to mourn, also recognizing the identity between the struggles of Athens and Sparta and the struggles of our modern world, and taking violently the contrary side to that of Mitford, being as great a democrat as Mitford was an aristocrat, wrote a reply, far above Mitford's history in power and learning, but being in its main characteristic almost identical, being above all things a book of vigorous political passion, written for persons who care for politics, and not, as almost all histories of antiquity are and must be, the book of a man who cares for scholarship more than for anything else, written mainly if not exclusively for scholars. And the effect of fundamental political discussion was the same in ancient as in modern times. The whole customary ways of thought were at once shaken by it, and shaken not only in the closets of philosophers, but in the common thought and daily business of ordinary men. The "liberation of humanity," as Goethe used to call it—the deliverance of men from the yoke of inherited usage, and of rigid, unquestionable law—was begun in Greece, and had many of its greatest effects, good and evil, on Greece. It is just because of the analogy between the controversies of that time and those of our times that someone has said: "Classical history is a part of modern history; it is mediaeval history only which is ancient."

If there had been no discussion of principle in Greece, probably she would still have produced works of art. Homer contains no such discussion. The speeches in the *Iliad*, which Mr. Gladstone, the most competent of living judges, maintains to be the finest ever composed by man, are not discussions of principle. There is no more tendency in them to critical disquisition than there is to political economy. In Herodotus you have the beginning of the age of discussion. He belongs in his essence to the age which is going out. He refers with reverence to established ordinance and fixed religion. Still, in his travels through Greece, he must have heard endless political arguments; and accordingly you can find in his book many incipient traces of abstract political disquisition. The discourses on democracy, aristocracy, and monarchy which he puts into the mouth of the Persian conspirators when the monarchy was vacant have justly been called absurd, as speeches supposed to have been spoken by those persons. No Asiatic ever thought of such things. You might as well imagine Saul or David speaking them as those to whom Herodotus attributes them. They are Greek speeches, full of free Greek discussion, and suggested by the experience, already considerable, of the Greeks in the results of discussion. The age of debate is beginning, and even Herodotus, the least of a wrangler of any man, and the most of a sweet and simple narrator, felt the effect. When we come to Thucydides, the results of discussion are as full as they have ever been; his light is pure, "dry light," free from the "humors" of habit, and purged from consecrated usage. As Grote's history often reads like a report to Parliament, so half Thucydides reads like a speech, or materials for a speech, in the Athenian Assembly. Of later times it is unnecessary to speak. Every page of Aristotle and Plato bears ample and indelible trace of the age of discussion in which they lived; and thought cannot possibly be freer. The deliverance of the speculative intellect from traditional and customary authority was altogether complete.

No doubt the "detachment" from prejudice, and the

subjection to reason, which I ascribe to ancient Athens, only went down a very little way among the population of it. Two great classes of the people, the slaves and women, were almost excluded from such qualities; even the free population doubtless contained a far greater proportion of very ignorant and very superstitious persons than we are in the habit of imagining. We fix our attention on the best specimens of Athenian culture in the books which have descended to us—and we forget that the corporate action of the Athenian people at various critical junctures exhibited the most gross superstition. Still, as far as the intellectual and cultivated part of society is concerned, the triumph of reason was complete; the minds of the highest philosophers were then as ready to obey evidence and reason as they have ever been since; probably they were more ready. The rule of custom over them at least had been wholly broken, and the primary conditions of intellectual progress were in that respect satisfied.

It may be said that I am giving too much weight to the classical idea of human development; that history contains the record of another progress as well; that in a certain sense there was progress in Judaea as well as in Athens. And unquestionably there was progress, but it was only progress upon a single subject. If we except religion and omit also all that the Jews had learned from foreigners, it may be doubted if there be much else new between the time of Samuel and that of Malachi. In religion there was progress, but without it there was not any. This was due to the cause of that progress. All over antiquity, all over the East, and over other parts of the world which preserve more or less nearly their ancient condition, there are two classes of religious teachers—one, the priests, the inheritors of past accredited inspiration; the other, the prophet, the possessor of a like present inspiration. Curtius* describes the distinction well in relation to the condition of Greece with which history first presents us:

> The mantic art is an institution totally different from the priesthood. It is based on the belief that the gods are in constant proximity to men, and in their government of the world, which comprehends every thing both great and small, will not disdain to manifest their will; nay, it seems necessary that, whenever any hitch has arisen in the moral system of the human world, this should also manifest itself by some sign in the world of nature, if only mortals are able to understand and avail themselves of these divine hints.
>
> For this a special capacity is requisite; not a capacity which can be learnt like a human art or science, but rather a peculiar state of grace in the case of single individuals and single families whose ears and eyes are opened to the divine revelations, and who participate more largely than the rest of mankind in the divine spirit. Accordingly it is their office and calling to assert themselves as organs of the divine will; they are justified in opposing their authority to every power of the world. On this head conflicts were unavoidable, and the reminiscences living in the Greek people, of the agency of a Tiresias and Calchas, prove how the Heroic kings experienced not only support and aid, but also

* [Ernst Curtius (1814–1896), German classicist. The following passage is from Volume II, Chapter IV of his *History of Greece*, translated by A. W. Ward (New York: Scribner, Armstrong, 1875), pages 7–8.—*Ed.*]

opposition and violent protests, from the mouths of the
men of prophecy.

In Judaea there was exactly the same opposition as elsewhere. All that is new comes from the prophets; all which
is old is retained by the priests. But the peculiarity of
Judaea—a peculiarity which I do not for a moment pretend that I can explain—is that the prophetic revelations
are, taken as a whole, indisputably improvements; that
they contain, as time goes on, at each succeeding epoch,
higher and better views of religion. But the peculiarity is
not to my present purpose. My point is that there is no
such spreading impetus in progress thus caused as there is
in progress caused by discussion. To receive a particular
conclusion upon the *ipse dixit*, upon the accepted authority of an admired instructor, is obviously not so vivifying
to the argumentative and questioning intellect as to argue
out conclusions for yourself. Accordingly the religious
progress caused by the prophets did not break down that
ancient code of authoritative usage. On the contrary, the
two combined. In each generation the conservative influence "built the sepulchers" and accepted the teaching
of past prophets, even while it was slaying and persecuting those who were living. But discussion and custom
cannot be thus combined; their "method," as modern
philosophers would say, is antagonistic. Accordingly, the
progress of the classical states gradually awakened the
whole intellect; that of Judaea was partial and improved
religion only. And, therefore, in a history of intellectual
progress, the classical fills the superior and the Jewish the
inferior place; just as in a special history of theology only,
the places of the two might be interchanged.

A second experiment has been tried on the same subject-matter. The characteristic of the Middle Ages may be approximately—though only approximately—described as a return to the period of authoritative usage and as an abandonment of the classical habit of independent and self-choosing thought. I do not for an instant mean that this is an exact description of the main mediaeval characteristic; nor can I discuss how far that characteristic was an advance upon those of previous times; its friends say it is far better than the peculiarities of the classical period; its enemies that it is far worse. But both friends and enemies will admit that the most marked feature of the Middle Ages may roughly be described as I have described it. And my point is that just as this mediaeval characteristic was that of a return to the essence of the customary epoch which had marked the pre-Athenian times, so it was dissolved much in the same manner as the influence of Athens, and other influences like it, claim to have dissolved that customary epoch.

The principal agent in breaking up the persistent mediaeval customs, which were so fixed that they seemed likely to last for ever, or till some historical catastrophe overwhelmed them, was the popular element in the ancient polity which was everywhere diffused in the Middle Ages. The Germanic tribes brought with them from their ancient dwelling-place a polity containing, like the classical, a king, a council, and a popular assembly; and wherever they went, they carried these elements and varied them, as force compelled or circumstances required. As far as England is concerned, the excellent dissertations of Mr. Freeman and Mr. Stubbs* have proved this in the

---

* [William Stubbs (1825–1901), important English historian and, from 1884, bishop of Chester.—*Ed.*]

amplest manner, and brought it home to persons who cannot claim to possess much antiquarian learning. The history of the English Constitution, as far as the world cares for it, is, in fact, the complex history of the popular element in this ancient polity, which was sometimes weaker and sometimes stronger, but which has never died out, has commonly possessed great though varying power, and is now entirely predominant. The history of this growth is the history of the English people; and the discussions about this constitution and the discussions within it, the controversies as to its structure and the controversies as to its true effects, have mainly trained the English political intellect, in so far as it is trained. But in much of Europe, and in England particularly, the influence of religion has been very different from what it was in antiquity. It has been an influence of discussion. Since Luther's time there has been a conviction more or less rooted that a man may by an intellectual process think out a religion for himself, and that, as the highest of all duties, he ought to do so. The influence of the political discussion and the influence of the religious discussion have been so long and so firmly combined, and have so effectually enforced one another, that the old notions of loyalty, and fealty, and authority, as they existed in the Middle Ages, have now over the best minds almost no effect.

It is true that the influence of discussion is not the only force which has produced this vast effect. Both in ancient and in modern times other forces cooperated with it. Trade, for example, is obviously a force which has done much to bring men of different customs and different beliefs into close contiguity, and has thus aided to change the customs and the beliefs of them all. Colonization is another such influence: it settles men among aborigines of alien race and usages, and it commonly compels the colonists not to be over-strict in the choice of their own elements; they are obliged to coalesce with and "adopt" useful bands and useful men, though their ancestral customs may not be identical, nay, though they may be, in fact, opposite to their own. In modern Europe the existence of a cosmopolite Church, claiming to be above nations, and really extending through nations, and the scattered remains of Roman law and Roman civilization cooperated with the liberating influence of political discussion. And so did other causes also. But perhaps in no case have these subsidiary causes alone been able to generate intellectual freedom; certainly in all the most remarkable cases the influence of discussion has presided at the creation of that freedom, and has been active and dominant in it.

No doubt apparent cases of exception may easily be found. It may be said that in the court of Augustus there was much general intellectual freedom, an almost entire detachment from ancient prejudice, but that there was no free political discussion at all. But, then, the ornaments of that time were derived from a time of great freedom: it was the republic which trained the men whom the empire ruled. The close congregation of most miscellaneous elements under the empire was, no doubt, of itself unfavorable to inherited prejudice, and favorable to intellectual exertion. Yet, except in the instance of the Church, which is a peculiar subject that requires a separate discussion, how little was added to what the republic left! The power of free interchange of ideas being wanting, the ideas themselves were barren. Also, no doubt, much intellectual freedom may emanate from countries of free political discussion, and penetrate to countries where that discussion is limited. Thus the intellectual freedom of France in the eighteenth century was in great part owing to the proximity of and incessant intercourse with England and Holland. Voltaire resided among us; and every page of the *Esprit des Lois* proves how much Montesquieu* learned from living here. But, of course, it was only part of the French culture which was so derived: the germ might be foreign, but the tissue was native. And very naturally, for it would be absurd to call the *ancien régime* a government without discussion: discussion abounded there, only, by reason of the bad form of the government, it was never sure with ease and certainty to affect political action. The despotism "tempered by epigram" was a government which permitted argument of licentious freedom within changing limits, and which was ruled by that argument spasmodically and practically, though not in name or consistently.

But though in the earliest and in the latest time government by discussion has been a principal organ for improving mankind, yet, from its origin, it is a plant of singular delicacy. At first the chances are much against its living. In the beginning the members of a free state are of necessity few. The essence of it requires that discussion shall be brought home to those members. But in early time, when writing is difficult, reading rare, and representation undiscovered, those who are to be guided by the discussion must hear it with their own ears, must be brought face to face with the orator, and must feel his in-

---

* [Charles-Louis de Secondat, Baron de Montesquieu (1689–1755), French political philosopher and jurist. *De l'Esprit des Lois* was first published in 1748.—*Ed.*]

fluence for themselves. The first free states were little towns, smaller than any political division which we now have, except the Republic of Andorre, which is a sort of vestige of them. It is in the marketplace of the country town, as we should now speak, and in petty matters concerning the market town, that discussion began, and thither all the long train of its consequences may be traced back. Some historical inquirers, like myself, can hardly look at such a place without some sentimental musing, poor and trivial as the thing seems. But such small towns are very feeble. Numbers in the earliest wars, as in the latest, are a main source of victory. And in early times one kind of state is very common and is exceedingly numerous. In every quarter of the globe we find great populations compacted by traditional custom and consecrated sentiment, which are ruled by some soldier—generally some soldier of a foreign tribe, who has conquered them, and, as it has been said, "vaulted on the back" of them, or whose ancestors have done so. These great populations, ruled by a single will, have, doubtless, trodden down and destroyed innumerable little cities who were just beginning their freedom.

In this way the Greek cities in Asia were subjected to the Persian power, and so *ought* the cities in Greece proper to have been subjected also. Every schoolboy must have felt that nothing but amazing folly and unmatched mismanagement saved Greece from conquest both in the time of Xerxes and in that of Darius. The fortunes of intellectual civilization were then at the mercy of what seems an insignificant probability. If the Persian leaders had only shown that decent skill and ordinary military prudence which it was likely they would show, Grecian freedom would have been at an end. Athens, like so many

Ionian cities on the other side of the Aegean, would have been absorbed into a great despotism; all we now remember her for we should not remember, for it would never have occurred. Her citizens might have been ingenious, and imitative, and clever; they could not certainly have been free and original. Rome was preserved from subjection to a great empire by her fortunate distance from one. The early wars of Rome are with cities like Rome—about equal in size, though inferior in valor. It was only when she had conquered Italy that she began to measure herself against Asiatic despotisms. She became great enough to beat them before she advanced far enough to contend with them. But such great good fortune was and must be rare. Unnumbered little cities which might have rivalled Rome or Athens doubtless perished without a sign long before history was imagined. The small size and slight strength of early free states made them always liable to easy destruction.

And their internal frailty is even greater. As soon as discussion begins, the savage propensities of men break forth; even in modern communities, where those propensities, too, have been weakened by ages of culture, and repressed by ages of obedience, as soon as a vital topic for discussion is well started the keenest and most violent passions break forth. Easily destroyed as are early free states by forces from without, they are even more liable to destruction by forces from within.

On this account such states are very rare in history. Upon the first view of the facts a speculation might even be set up that they were peculiar to a particular race. By far the most important free institutions, and the only ones which have left living representatives in the world, are the offspring either of the first constitutions of the classical nations or of the first constitutions of the Germanic nations. All living freedom runs back to them, and those truths which at first sight would seem the whole of historical freedom can be traced to them. And both the Germanic and the classical nations belong to what ethnologists call the Aryan race. Plausibly it might be argued that the power of forming free states was superior in and peculiar to that family of mankind. But unfortunately for this easy theory, the facts are inconsistent with it. In the first place, all the so-called Aryan race certainly is not free. The Eastern Aryans—those, for example, who speak languages derived from the Sanskrit—are amongst the most slavish divisions of mankind. To offer the Bengalese a free constitution, and to expect them to work one, would be the maximum of human folly. There then must be something else besides Aryan descent which is necessary to fit men for discussion and train them for liberty; and, what is worse for the argument we are opposing, some non-Aryan races have been capable of freedom. Carthage, for example, was a Semitic republic. We do not know all the details of its constitution, but we know enough for our present purpose. We know that it was a government in which many proposers took part, and under which discussion was constant, active, and conclusive. No doubt Tyre, the parent city of Carthage, the other colonies of Tyre besides Carthage, and the colonies of Carthage were all as free as Carthage. We have thus a whole group of ancient republics of non-Aryan race, and one which, being more ancient than the classical republics, could not have borrowed from or imitated them. So that the theory which would make government by discussion the exclusive patrimony of a single race of mankind is on the face of it untenable.

I am not prepared with any simple counter theory. I cannot profess to explain completely why a very small minimum of mankind were, as long as we know of them, possessed of a polity which as time went on suggested discussions of principle, and why the great majority of mankind had nothing like it. This is almost as hopeless as asking why Milton was a genius and why Bacon was a philosopher. Indeed, it is the same, because the causes which give birth to the startling varieties of individual character and those which give birth to similar varieties of national character are, in fact, the same. I have, indeed, endeavored to show that a marked type of individual character once originating in a nation and once strongly preferred by it is likely to be fixed on it and to be permanent in it, from causes which were stated. Granted the beginning of the type, we may, I think, explain its development and aggravation; but we cannot in the least explain why the incipient type of curious characters broke out, if I may so say, in one place rather than in another. Climate and "physical" surroundings, in the largest sense, have unquestionably much influence; they are one factor in the cause, but they are not the only factor; for we find most dissimilar races of men living in the same climate and affected by the same surroundings, and we have every reason to believe that those unlike races have so lived as neighbors for ages. The cause of types must be something outside the tribe acting on something within—something inherited by the tribe. But what that something is I do not know that anyone can in the least explain.

The following conditions may, I think, be historically traced to the nation capable of a polity, which suggests principles for discussion, and so leads to progress. First, the nation must possess the *patria potestas** in some form so marked as to give family life distinctness and precision, and to make a home education and a home discipline probable and possible. While descent is traced only through the mother, and while the family is therefore a vague entity, no progress to a high polity is possible. Secondly, that polity would seem to have been created very gradually; by the aggregation of families into clans or *gentes*, and of clans into nations, and then again by the widening of nations, so as to include circumjacent outsiders, as well as the first compact and sacred group—the number of parties to a discussion was at first augmented very slowly. Thirdly, the number of "open" subjects, as we should say nowadays—that is, of subjects on which public opinion was optional, and on which discussion was admitted, was at first very small. Custom ruled everything originally, and the area of free argument was enlarged but very slowly. If I am at all right, that area could only be enlarged thus slowly, for custom was in early days the cement of society, and if you suddenly questioned such custom you would destroy society. But though the existence of these conditions may be traced historically, and though the reason of them may be explained philosophically, they do not completely solve the question why some nations have the polity and some not; on the contrary, they plainly leave a large "residual phenomenon" unexplained and unknown.

II

In this manner politics or discussion broke up the old bonds of custom which were now strangling mankind,

* [*Patria potestas*: native power.—*Ed.*]

though they had once aided and helped it. But this is only one of the many gifts which those polities have conferred, are conferring, and will confer on mankind. I am not going to write a eulogium on liberty, but I wish to set down three points which have not been sufficiently noticed.

Civilized ages inherit the human nature which was victorious in barbarous ages, and that nature is, in many respects, not at all suited to civilized circumstances. A main and principal excellence in the early times of the human races is the impulse to action. The problems before men are then plain and simple. The man who works hardest, the man who kills the most deer, the man who catches the most fish—even later on, the man who tends the largest herds, or the man who tills the largest field—is the man who succeeds; the nation which is quickest to kill its enemies, or which kills most of its enemies, is the nation which succeeds. All the inducements of early society tend to foster immediate action; all its penalties fall on the man who pauses; the traditional wisdom of those times was never weary of inculcating that "delays are dangerous," and that the sluggish man— the man "who roasteth not that which he took in hunting"—will not prosper on the earth, and indeed will very soon perish out of it. And in consequence an inability to stay quiet, an irritable desire to act directly, is one of the most conspicuous failings of mankind.

Pascal* said that most of the evils of life arose from "man's being unable to sit still in a room"; and though I

* [Blaise Pascal (1623–1662), French philosopher, mathematician, scientist, and theologian. The famous passage to which Bagehot alludes is from Pascal's posthumously pub-

do not go that length, it is certain that we should have been a far wiser race than we are if we had been readier to sit quiet—we should have known much better the way in which it was best to act when we came to act. The rise of physical science, the first great body of practical truth provable to all men, exemplifies this in the plainest way. If it had not been for quiet people, who sat still and studied the sections of the cone, if other quiet people had not sat still and studied the theory of infinitesimals, or other quiet people had not sat still and worked out the doctrine of chances, the most "dreamy moonshine," as the purely practical mind would consider, of all human pursuits; if "idle star-gazers" had not watched long and carefully the motions of the heavenly bodies—our modern astronomy would have been impossible, and without our astronomy "our ships, our colonies, our seamen," all which makes modern life modern life, could not have existed. Ages of sedentary, quiet-thinking people were required before that noisy existence began, and without those pale preliminary students it never could have been brought into being. And nine-tenths of modern science is in this respect the same: it is the produce of men whom their contemporaries thought dreamers—who were laughed at for caring for what did not concern them—who, as the proverb went, "walked into a well from looking at the stars"— who were believed to be useless, if anyone could be such. And the conclusion is plain that if there had been more such people, if the world had not laughed at those there

---

lished *Pensées*: "J'ai découvert que tout le malheur des hommes vient d'une seule chose, qui est de ne savoir pas demeurer en repos, dans une chambre" (§ 139).—*Ed.*]

were, if rather it had encouraged them, there would have been a great accumulation of proved science ages before there was. It was the irritable activity, the "wish to be doing something," that prevented it. Most men inherited a nature too eager and too restless to be quiet and find out things; and even worse—with their idle clamor they "disturbed the brooding hen," they would not let those be quiet who wished to be so, and out of whose calm thought much good might have come forth.

If we consider how much science has done and how much it is doing for mankind, and if the over-activity of men is proved to be the cause why science came so late into the world, and is so small and scanty still, that will convince most people that our over-activity is a very great evil. But this is only part, and perhaps not the greatest part of the harm that over-activity does. As I have said, it is inherited from times when life was simple, objects were plain, and quick action generally led to desirable ends. If A kills B before B kills A, then A survives, and the human race is a race of A's. But the issues of life are plain no longer. To act rightly in modern society requires a great deal of previous study, a great deal of assimilated information, a great deal of sharpened imagination; and these prerequisites of sound action require much time, and, I was going to say, much "lying in the sun," a long period of "mere passiveness." Even the art of killing one another, which at first particularly trained men to be quick, now requires them to be slow. A hasty general is the worst of generals nowadays; the best is a sort of von Moltke,* who is passive if any man ever was passive; who is "silent in

* [Helmut Karl Bernhard von Moltke (1800–1891), Prussian field marshal and brilliant military tactician.—*Ed.*]

seven languages"; who possesses more and better ac-
cumulated information as to the best way of killing
people than anyone who ever lived. This man plays a
restrained and considerate game of chess with his enemy.
I wish the art of benefiting men had kept pace with the
art of destroying them; for though war has become slow,
philanthropy has remained hasty. The most melancholy of
human reflections, perhaps, is that, on the whole, it is a
question whether the benevolence of mankind does most
good or harm. Great good, no doubt, philanthropy does,
but then it also does great evil. It augments so much vice,
it multiplies so much suffering, it brings to life such great
populations to suffer and to be vicious, that it is open to
argument whether it be or be not an evil to the world,
and this is entirely because excellent people fancy that
they can do much by rapid action—that they will most
benefit the world when they most relieve their own
feelings; that as soon as an evil is seen, "something"
ought to be done to stay and prevent it. One may incline
to hope that the balance of good over evil is in favor of
benevolence; one can hardly bear to think that it is not
so; but anyhow it is certain that there is a most heavy
debit of evil, and that this burden might almost all have
been spared us if philanthropists as well as others had not
inherited from their barbarous forefathers a wild passion
for instant action.

Even in commerce, which is now the main occupation
of mankind, and one in which there is a ready test of success and failure wanting in many higher pursuits, the
same disposition to excessive action is very apparent to
careful observers. Part of every mania is caused by the
impossibility to get people to confine themselves to the
amount of business for which their capital is sufficient,

and in which they can engage safely. In some degree, of course, this is caused by the wish to get rich; but in a considerable degree, too, by the mere love of activity. There is a greater propensity to action in such men than they have the means of gratifying. Operations with their own capital will only occupy four hours of the day, and they wish to be active and to be industrious for eight hours, and so they are ruined. If they could only have sat idle the other four hours, they would have been rich men. The amusements of mankind, at least of the English part of mankind, teach the same lesson. Our shooting, our hunting, our traveling, our climbing have become laborious pursuits. It is a common saying abroad that "an Englishman's notion of a holiday is a fatiguing journey"; and this is only another way of saying that the immense energy and activity which have given us our place in the world have in many cases descended to those who do not find in modern life any mode of using that activity, and of venting that energy.

Even the abstract speculations of mankind bear conspicuous traces of the same excessive impulse. Every sort of philosophy has been systematized, and yet as these philosophies utterly contradict one another, most of them cannot be true. Unproved abstract principles without number have been eagerly caught up by sanguine men, and then carefully spun out into books and theories, which were to explain the whole world. But the world goes clear against these abstractions, and it must do so, as they require it to go in antagonistic directions. The mass of a system attracts the young and impresses the unwary; but cultivated people are very dubious about it. They are ready to receive hints and suggestions, and the smallest real truth is ever welcome. But a large book of deductive philosophy is much to be suspected. No doubt the deductions may be right; in most writers they are so; but where did the premises come from? Who is sure that they are the whole truth, and nothing but the truth, of the matter in hand? Who is not almost sure beforehand that they will contain a strange mixture of truth and error, and therefore that it will not be worth while to spend life in reasoning over their consequences? In a word, the superfluous energy of mankind has flowed over into philosophy, and has worked into big systems what should have been left as little suggestions.

And if the old systems of thought are not true *as* systems, neither is the new revolt from them to be trusted in its whole vigor. There is the same original vice in that also. There is an excessive energy in revolutions if there is such energy anywhere. The passion for action is quite as ready to pull down as to build up; probably it is more ready, for the task is easier.

> Old things need not be therefore true,
> O brother men, nor yet the new;
> Ah, still awhile the old thought retain,
> And yet consider it again.

But this is exactly what the human mind will not do. It will act somehow at once. It will not "consider it again."

But it will be said: What has government by discussion to do with these things? Will it prevent them, or even mitigate them? It can and does do both in the very plainest way. If you want to stop instant and immediate action, always make it a condition that the action shall not begin till a considerable number of persons have talked over it, and have agreed on it. If those persons be people of different temperaments, different ideas, and different educations, you have an almost infallible security that nothing, or almost nothing, will be done with excessive rapidity. Each kind of persons will have their spokesman; each spokesman will have his characteristic objection, and each his characteristic counter-proposition, and so in the end nothing will probably be done, or at least only the minimum which is plainly urgent. In many cases this delay may be dangerous; in many cases quick action will be preferable. A campaign, as Macaulay well says, cannot be directed by a "debating society"; and many other kinds of action also require a single and absolute general. But for the purpose now in hand—that of preventing hasty action, and ensuring elaborate consideration—there is no device like a polity of discussion.

The enemies of this object—the people who want to act quickly—see this very distinctly. They are for ever explaining that the present is "an age of committees," that the committees do nothing, that all evaporates in talk. Their great enemy is parliamentary government; they call it, after Mr. Carlyle, the "national palaver"; they add up the hours that are consumed in it, and the speeches which are made in it, and they sigh for a time when England might again be ruled, as it once was, by a Cromwell*— that is, when an eager, absolute man might do exactly what other eager men wished, and do it immediately. All these invectives are perpetual and many-sided; they come from philosophers, each of whom wants some new scheme tried; from philanthropists, who want some evil abated; from revolutionists, who want some old institu-

* [Oliver Cromwell (1599–1658), Puritan solider, politician, and—after engineering the execution of Charles I—Lord Protector of England (1653–1658).—*Ed.*]

tion destroyed; from new eraists, who want their new era started forthwith. And they all are distinct admissions that a polity of discussion is the greatest hindrance to the inherited mistake of human nature, to the desire to act promptly, which in a simple age is so excellent, but which in a later and complex time leads to so much evil.

The same accusation against our age sometimes takes a more general form. It is alleged that our energies are diminishing; that ordinary and average men have not the quick determination nowadays which they used to have when the world was younger; that not only do not committees and parliaments act with rapid decisiveness, but that no one now so acts. And I hope that in fact this is true, for according to me, it proves that the hereditary barbaric impulse is decaying and dying out. So far from thinking the quality attributed to us a defect, I wish that those who complain of it were far more right than I much fear they are. Still, certainly, eager and violent action is somewhat diminished, though only by a small fraction of what it ought to be. And I believe that this is in great part due, in England at least, to our government by discussion, which has fostered a general intellectual tone, a diffused disposition to weigh evidence, a conviction that much may be said on every side of everything which the elder and more fanatic ages of the world wanted. This is the real reason why our energies seem so much less than those of our fathers. When we have a definite end in view, which we know we want, and which we think we know how to obtain, we can act well enough. The campaigns of our soldiers are as energetic as any campaigns ever were; the speculations of our merchants have greater promptitude, greater audacity, greater vigor than any such speculations ever had before. In old times a few ideas got possession of men and communities, but this is happily now possible no longer. We see how incomplete these old ideas were; how almost by chance one seized on one nation, and another on another; how often one set of men have persecuted another set for opinions on subjects of which neither, we now perceive, knew anything. It might be well if a greater number of effectual demonstrations existed among mankind; but while no such demonstrations exist, and while the evidence which completely convinces one man seems to another trifling and insufficient, let us recognize the plain position of inevitable doubt. Let us not be bigots with a doubt, and persecutors without a creed. We are beginning to see this, and we are railed at for so beginning. But it is a great benefit, and it is to the incessant prevalence of detective discussion that our doubts are due; and much of that discussion is due to the long existence of a government requiring constant debates, written and oral.

This is one of the unrecognized benefits of free government, one of the modes in which it counteracts the excessive inherited impulses of humanity. There is another also for which it does the same, but which I can only touch delicately, and which at first sight will seem ridiculous. The most successful races, other things being equal, are those which multiply the fastest. In the conflicts of mankind numbers have ever been a great power. The most numerous group has always had an advantage over the less numerous, and the fastest breeding group has always tended to be the most numerous. In consequence, human nature has descended into a comparatively uncontentious civilization, with a desire far in excess of what is needed; with a "felt want," as political economists would say, altogether greater than the "real want."

A walk in London is all which is necessary to establish this. "The great sin of great cities" is one vast evil consequent upon it. And who is to reckon up how much these words mean? How many spoiled lives, how many broken hearts, how many wasted bodies, how many ruined minds, how much misery pretending to be gay, how much gaiety feeling itself to be miserable, how much after mental pain, how much eating and transmitted disease. And in the moral part of the world, how many minds are racked by incessant anxiety, how many thoughtful imaginations which might have left something to mankind are debased to mean cares, how much every successive generation sacrifices to the next, how little does any of them make of itself in comparison with what might be! And how many Irelands have there been in the world where men would have been contented and happy if they had only been fewer; how many more Irelands would there have been if the intrusive numbers had not been kept down by infanticide and vice and misery! How painful is the conclusion that it is dubious whether all the machines and inventions of mankind "have yet lightened the day's labor of a human being"! They have enabled more people to exist, but these people work just as hard and are just as mean and miserable as the elder and the fewer.

But it will be said of this passion just as it was said of the passion of activity: Granted that it is in excess, how can you say, how on earth can anyone say, that government by discussion can in any way cure or diminish it? Cure this evil that government certainly will not; but tend to diminish it—I think it does and may. To show that I am not making premises to support a conclusion so abnormal, I will quote a passage from Mr. Spencer, the philosopher who has done most to illustrate this subject:

> That future progress of civilization which the never-ceasing pressure of population must produce, will be accompanied by an enhanced cost of individuation, both in structure and function; and more especially in nervous structure and function. The peaceful struggle for existence in societies ever growing more crowded and more complicated, must have for its concomitant an increase of the great nervous centers in mass, in complexity, in activity. The larger body of emotion needed as a fountain of energy for men who have to hold their places and rear their families under the intensifying competition of social life, is, other things equal, the correlative of a larger brain. Those higher feelings presupposed by the better self-regulation which, in a better society, can alone enable the individual to leave a persistent posterity, are, other things equal, the correlatives of a more complex brain; as are also those more numerous, more varied, more general, and more abstract ideas, which must also become increasingly requisite for successful life as society advances. And the genesis of this larger quantity of feeling and thought in a brain thus augmented in size and developed in structure, is, other things equal, the correlative of a greater wear of nervous tissue and greater consumption of materials to repair it. So that both in original cost of construction and in subsequent cost of working, the nervous system must become a heavier tax on the organism. Already the brain of the civilized man is larger by nearly thirty per cent. than the brain of the savage. Already, too, it presents an in-

creased heterogeneity specially in the distribution of its convolutions. And further changes like these which have taken place under the discipline of civilized life, we infer will continue to take place. . . . But everywhere and always, evolution is antagonistic to procreative dissolution. Whether it be in greater growth of the organs which subserve self-maintenance, whether it be in their added complexity of structure, or whether it be in their higher activity, the abstraction of the required materials implies a diminished reserve of materials for race-maintenance. And we have seen reason to believe that this antagonism between individuation and genesis becomes unusually marked where the nervous system is concerned, because of the costliness of nervous structure and function. In §346 was pointed out the apparent connection between high cerebral development and prolonged delay of sexual maturity; and in §§366, 367, the evidence went to show that where exceptional fertility exists there is sluggishness of mind, and that where there has been during education excessive expenditure in mental action, there frequently follows a complete or partial infertility. Hence the particular kind of further evolution which Man is hereafter to undergo, is one which, more than any other, may be expected to cause a decline in his power of reproduction.*

This means that men who have to live an intellectual life, or who can be induced to lead one, will be likely not to have so many children as they would otherwise have

* [From Volume II, Chapter XIII of *The Principles of Biology* (New York: D. Appleton, 1867), pages 529–530.—*Ed.*]

had. In particular cases this may not be true; such men may even have many children, they may be men in all ways of unusual power and vigor. But they will not have their maximum of posterity—will not have so many as they would have had if they had been careless or thoughtless men; and so, upon an average, the issue of such intellectualized men will be less numerous than those of the unintellectual.

Now, supposing this philosophical doctrine to be true —and the best philosophers, I think, believe it—its application to the case in hand is plain. Nothing promotes intellect like intellectual discussion, and nothing promotes intellectual discussion so much as government by discussion. The perpetual atmosphere of intellectual inquiry acts powerfully, as everyone may see by looking about him in London, upon the constitution both of men and women. There is only a certain *quantum* of power in each of our race; if it goes in one way it is spent, and cannot go in another. The intellectual atmosphere abstracts strength to intellectual matters; it tends to divert that strength which the circumstances of early society directed to the multiplication of numbers; and as a polity of discussion tends, above all things, to produce an intellectual atmosphere, the two things which seemed so far off have been shown to be near, and free government has, in a second case, been shown to tend to cure an inherited excess of human nature.

Lastly, a polity of discussion not only tends to diminish our inherited defects, but also, in one case at least, to augment a heritable excellence. It tends to strengthen and increase a subtle quality or combination of qualities singularly useful in practical life—a quality which it is not easy to describe exactly, and the issues of which it would require not a remnant of an essay, but a whole essay to elucidate completely. This quality I call *animated moderation*.

If anyone were asked to describe what it is which distinguishes the writings of a man of genius who is also a great man of the world from all other writings, I think he would use these same words, "animated moderation." He would say that such writings are never slow, are never excessive, are never exaggerated; that they are always instinct with judgment, and yet that judgment is never a dull judgment; that they have as much spirit in them as would go to make a wild writer, and yet that every line of them is the product of a sane and sound writer. The best and almost perfect instance of this in English is Scott. Homer was perfect in it, as far as we can judge; Shakespeare is often perfect in it for long together, though then, from the defects of a bad education and a vicious age, all at once he loses himself in excesses. Still, Homer, and Shakespeare at his best, and Scott, though in other respects so unequal to them, have this remarkable quality in common—this union of life with measure, of spirit with reasonableness.

In action it is equally this quality in which the English —at least so I claim it for them—excel all other nations. There is an infinite deal to be laid against us, and as we are unpopular with most others, and as we are always grumbling at ourselves, there is no want of people to say it. But, after all, in a certain sense, England is a success in the world; her career has had many faults, but still it has been a fine and winning career upon the whole. And this on account of the exact possession of this particular quality. What is the making of a successful merchant? That he has plenty of energy, and yet that he does not go too far. And if you ask for a description of a great practical Englishman, you will be sure to have this, or something like it: "Oh, he has plenty of go in him; but he knows when to pull up." He may have all other defects in him; he may be coarse, he may be illiterate, he may be stupid to talk to; still this great union of spur and bridle, of energy and moderation, will remain to him. Probably he will hardly be able to explain why he stops when he does stop, or why he continued to move as long as he, in fact, moved; but still, as by a rough instinct, he pulls up pretty much where he should, though he was going at such a pace before.

There is no better example of this quality in English statesmen than Lord Palmerston. There are, of course, many most serious accusations to be made against him. The sort of homage with which he was regarded in the last years of his life has passed away; the spell is broken, and the magic cannot be again revived. We may think that his information was meager, that his imagination was narrow, that his aims were short-sighted and faulty. But though we may often object to his objects, we rarely find much to criticize in his means. "He went," it has been said, "with a great swing"; but he never tumbled over; he always managed to pull up "before there was any danger." He was an odd man to have inherited Hampden's motto;* still, in fact, there was a great trace in him of *mediocria firma*—as much, probably, as there could be in anyone of such great vivacity and buoyancy.

It is plain that this is a quality which as much as, if not

---

* [John Hampden (1594–1643), leader of the parliamentary opposition under Charles I. His motto means "steadfast moderation."—*Ed.*]

more than, any other multiplies good results in practical life. It enables men to see what is good; it gives them intellect enough for sufficient perception; but it does not make men all intellect; it does not "sickly them o'er with the pale cast of thought"; it enables them to do the good things they see to be good, as well as to see that they are good. And it is plain that a government by popular discussion tends to produce this quality. A strongly idiosyncratic mind, violently disposed to extremes of opinion, is soon weeded out of political life, and a bodiless thinker, an ineffectual scholar, cannot even live there for a day. A vigorous moderateness in mind and body is the rule of a polity which works by discussion; and, upon the whole, it is the kind of temper most suited to the active life of such a being as man in such a world as the present one.

These three great benefits of free government, though great, are entirely secondary to its continued usefulness in the mode in which it originally was useful. The first great benefit was the deliverance of mankind from the superannuated yoke of customary law, by the gradual development of an inquisitive originality. And it continues to produce that effect upon persons apparently far remote from its influence, and on subjects with which it has nothing to do. Thus Mr. Mundella,* a most experienced and capable judge, tells us that the English artisan, though so much less sober, less instructed, and less refined than the artisans of some other countries, is yet more inventive than any other artisan. The master will get more good suggestions from him than from any other.

* [Anthony John Mundella (1825–1897), British Liberal politician.—*Ed.*]

Again, upon plausible grounds—looking, for example, to the position of Locke and Newton in the science of the last century, and to that of Darwin in our own—it may be argued that there is some quality in English thought which makes them strike out as many, if not more, first-rate and original suggestions as nations of greater scientific culture and more diffused scientific interest. In both cases I believe the reason of the English originality to be that government by discussion quickens and enlivens thought all through society; that it makes people think no harm may come of thinking; that in England this force has long been operating, and so it has developed more of all kinds of people ready to use their mental energy in their own way, and not ready to use it in any other way, than a despotic government. And so rare is great originality among mankind, and so great are its fruits, that this one benefit of free government probably outweighs what are in many cases its accessory evils. Of itself it justifies, or goes far to justify, our saying with Montesquieu: "Whatever be the cost of this glorious liberty, we must be content to pay it to heaven."*

* [See Montesquieu, *The Spirit of the Laws*, Volume I, Book XIX, Chapter 27, "How the Laws Contribute to Form the Manners, Customs, and Character of a Nation."—*Ed.*]

6

Verifiable Progress
Politically Considered

T HE ORIGINAL publication of these essays was interrupted by serious illness and by long consequent ill-
health, and now that I am putting them together I wish to
add another which shall shortly explain the main thread
of the argument which they contain. In doing so there is a
risk of tedious repetition, but on a subject both obscure
and important, any defect is better than an appearance of
vagueness.

In a former essay I attempted to show that slighter
causes than is commonly thought may change a nation
from the stationary to the progressive state of civilization,
and from the stationary to the degrading. Commonly the
effect of the agent is looked on in the wrong way. It is
considered as operating on every individual in the nation,
and it is assumed, or half-assumed, that it is only the effect which the agent directly produces on everyone that
need be considered. But besides this diffused effect of the
first impact of the cause, there is a second effect, always
considerable, and commonly more potent—a new *model*
in character is created for the nation; those characters
which resemble it are encouraged and multiplied; those
contrasted with it are persecuted and made fewer. In a

generation or two the look of the nation becomes quite different; the characteristic men who stand out are different, the men imitated are different; the result of the imitation is different. A lazy nation may be changed into an industrious, a rich into a poor, a religious into a profane, as if by magic, if any single cause, though slight, or any combination of causes, however subtle, is strong enough to change the favorite and detested types of character.

This principle will, I think, help us in trying to solve the question why so few nations have progressed, though to us progress seems so natural—what is the cause or set of causes which have prevented that progress in the vast majority of cases, and produced it in the feeble minority. But there is a preliminary difficulty: What is progress, and what is decline? Even in the animal world there is no applicable rule accepted by physiologists which settles what animals are higher or lower than others; there are controversies about it. Still more, then, in the more complex combinations and politics of human beings it is likely to be hard to find an agreed criterion for saying which nation is before another, or what age of a nation was marching forward and which was falling back. Archbishop Manning* would have one rule of progress and decline; Professor Huxley, in most important points, quite an opposite rule; what one would set down as an advance, the other would set down as a retreat. Each has a distinct end which he wishes and a distinct calamity which he fears, but the desire of the one is pretty near the fear of the other; books would not hold the controversy

---

* [Henry Edward Manning (1808–1892), Anglican churchman and, after his conversion, Roman Catholic cardinal.—*Ed.*]

between them. Again, in art, who is to settle what is advance and what decline? Would Mr. Ruskin* agree with anyone else on this subject, would he even agree with himself, or could any common inquirer venture to say whether he was right or wrong?

I am afraid that I must, as Sir William Hamilton‡ used to say, "truncate a problem which I cannot solve." I must decline to sit in judgment on disputed points of art, morals, or religion. But without so doing I think there is such a thing as "verifiable progress," if we may say so; that is, progress which ninety-nine hundredths or more of mankind will admit to be such, against which there is no established or organized opposition creed, and the objectors to which, essentially varying in opinion themselves, and believing one one thing and another the reverse, may be safely and altogether rejected.

Let us consider in what a village of English colonists is superior to a tribe of Australian natives who roam about them. Indisputably in one, and that a main sense, they are superior. They can beat the Australians in war when they like; they can take from them anything they like, and kill any of them they choose. As a rule, in all the outlying and uncontested districts of the world, the aboriginal native lies at the mercy of the intruding European. Nor is this all. Indisputably in the English village there are more means of happiness, a greater accumulation of the instruments of enjoyment, than in the Australian tribe. The English have all manner of books, utensils, and machines

* [John Ruskin (1819–1900), a pre-eminent Victorian art critic and social theorist.—*Ed.*]

‡ [Sir William Hamilton (1788–1856), British philosopher and logician.—*Ed.*]

which the others do not use, value, or understand. And in addition, and beyond particular inventions, there is a general strength which is capable of being used in conquering a thousand difficulties, and is an abiding source of happiness, because those who possess it always feel that they can use it.

If we omit the higher but disputed topics of morals and religion, we shall find, I think, that the plainer and agreed-on superiorities of the Englishmen are these: first, that they have a greater command over the powers of nature upon the whole. Though they may fall short of individual Australians in certain feats of petty skill, though they may not throw the boomerang as well, or light a fire with earthsticks as well, yet on the whole twenty Englishmen with their implements and skill can change the material world immeasurably more than twenty Australians and their machines. Secondly, that this power is not external only; it is also internal. The English not only possess better machines for moving nature, but are themselves better machines. Mr. Babbage* taught us years ago that one great use of machinery was not to augment the force of man, but to register and regulate the power of man; and this in a thousand ways civilized man can do, and is ready to do, better and more precisely than the barbarian. Thirdly, civilized man not only has greater powers over nature, but knows better how to use them, and by better I here mean better for the health and comfort of his present body and mind. He can lay up for old age, which a savage having no durable means of sus-

* [Charles Babbage (1792–1871), English mathematician and inventor, attempted to perfect a mechanical calculating machine, a forerunner of the modern computer.—Ed.]

tenance cannot; he is ready to lay up because he can distinctly foresee the future, which the vague-minded savage cannot; he is mainly desirous of gentle, continuous pleasure, whereas the barbarian likes wild excitement, and longs for stupefying repletion. Much, if not all, of these three ways may be summed up in Mr. Spencer's phrase, that progress is an increase of adaptation of man to his environment—that is, of his internal powers and wishes to his external lot and life. Something of it too is expressed in the old pagan idea "mens sana in corpore sano."* And I think this sort of progress may be fairly investigated quite separately, as it is progress in a sort of good everyone worth reckoning with admits and agrees in. No doubt there will remain people like the aged savage who in his old age went back to his savage tribe and said that he had "tried civilization for forty years, and it was not worth the trouble." But we need not take account of the mistaken ideas of unfit men and beaten races. On the whole the plainer sort of civilization, the simpler moral training, and the more elementary education are plain benefits. And though there may be doubt as to the edges of the conception, yet there certainly is a broad road of "verifiable progress" which not only discoverers and admirers will like, but which all those who come upon it will use and value.

Unless some kind of abstraction like this is made in the subject, the great problem "What causes progress?" will, I am confident, long remain unsolved. Unless we are content to solve simple problems first, the whole history of

* ["A healthy mind in a healthy body." The proverbial tag comes from the Roman satirist Juvenal, *Satires* 10:356. —Ed.]

philosophy teaches that we shall never solve hard problems. This is the maxim of scientific humility so often insisted on by the highest inquirers that, in investigations, as in life, those "who exalt themselves shall be abased, and those who humble themselves shall be exalted";* and though we may seem mean only to look for the laws of plain comfort and simple present happiness, yet we must work out that simple case first, before we encounter the incredibly harder additional difficulties of the higher art, morals, and religion.

The difficulty of solving the problem even thus limited is exceedingly great. The most palpable facts are exactly the contrary to what we should expect. Lord Macaulay tells us that "In every experimental science there is a tendency towards perfection. In every human being there is a tendency to ameliorate his condition"; and these two principles operating everywhere and always might well have been expected to "carry mankind rapidly forward." Indeed, taking verifiable progress in the sense which has just been given to it, we may say that nature gives a prize to every single step in it. Everyone that makes an invention that benefits himself or those around him is likely to be more comfortable himself and to be more respected by those around him. To produce new things "serviceable to man's life and conducive to man's estate" is, we should say, likely to bring increased happiness to the producer. It often brings immense reward certainly now; a new form of good steel pen, a way of making some kind of clothes a little better or a little cheaper, have brought men great fortunes. And there is the same kind of prize for industrial improvement in the earliest times as in the latest;

* [Luke XIV:11.—*Ed.*]

though the benefits so obtainable in early society are poor indeed in comparison with those of advanced society. Nature is like a schoolmaster, at least in this, she gives her finest prizes to her high and most instructed classes. Still, even in the earliest society, nature helps those who can help themselves, and helps them very much.

All this should have made the progress of mankind—progress at least in this limited sense exceedingly common; but in fact any progress is extremely rare. As a rule (and as has been insisted on before) a stationary state is by far the most frequent condition of man, as far as history describes that condition; the progressive state is only a rare and an occasional exception.

Before history began there must have been in the nation which writes it much progress; else there could have been no history. It is a great advance in civilization to be able to describe the common facts of life, and perhaps, if we were to examine it, we should find that it was at least an equal advance to wish to describe them. But very few races have made this step of progress; very few have been capable even of the meanest sort of history; and as for writing such a history as that of Thucydides, most nations could as soon have constructed a planet. When history begins to record, she finds most of the races incapable of history, arrested, unprogressive, and pretty much where they are now.

Why, then, have not the obvious and natural causes of progress (as we should call them) produced those obvious and natural effects? Why have the real fortunes of mankind been so different from the fortunes which we should expect? This is the problem which in various forms I have taken up in these papers, and this is the outline of the solution which I have attempted to propose.

The progress of *man* requires the cooperation of *men* for its development. That which any one man or any one family could invent for themselves is obviously exceedingly limited. And even if this were not true, isolated progress could never be traced. The rudest sort of cooperative society, the lowest tribe and the feeblest government, is so much stronger than isolated man that isolated man (if he ever existed in any shape which could be called man) might very easily have ceased to exist. The first principle of the subject is that man can only make progress in "cooperative groups"; I might say tribes and nations, but I use the less common word because few people would at once see that tribes and nations *are* cooperative groups, and that it is their being so which makes their value; that unless you can make a strong cooperative bond, your society will be conquered and killed out by some other society which has such a bond; and the second principle is that the members of such a group should be similar enough to one another to cooperate easily and readily together. The cooperation in all such cases depends on a *felt union* of heart and spirit; and this is only felt when there is a great degree of real likeness in mind and feeling, however that likeness may have been attained.

This needful cooperation and this requisite likeness I believe to have been produced by one of the strongest yokes (as we should think if it were to be reimposed now) and the most terrible tyrannies ever known among men—the authority of "customary law." In its earlier stage this is no pleasant power no "rose-water" authority, as Carlyle would have called it—but a stern, incessant, implacable rule. And the rule is often of most childish origin, beginning in a casual superstition or local accident. "These people," says Captain Palmer* of the Fiji, "are very conservative. A chief was one day going over a mountain-path followed by a long string of his people, when he happened to stumble and fall; all the rest of the people immediately did the same except one man, who was set upon by the rest to know whether he considered himself better than the chief." What can be worse than a life regulated by that sort of obedience, and that sort of imitation? This is, of course, a bad specimen, but the nature of customary law as we everywhere find it in its earliest stages is that of coarse casual comprehensive usage, beginning we cannot tell how, deciding we cannot tell why, but ruling everyone in almost every action with an inflexible grasp.

The necessity of thus forming cooperative groups by fixed customs explains the necessity of isolation in early society. As a matter of fact all great nations have been prepared in privacy and in secret. They have been composed far away from all distraction. Greece, Rome, Judaea, were framed each by itself, and the antipathy of each to men of different race and different speech is one of their most marked peculiarities, and quite their strongest common property. And the instinct of early ages is a right guide for the needs of early ages. Intercourse with foreigners then broke down in states the fixed rules which were forming their characters, so as to be a cause of weak fiber of mind, of desultory and unsettled action; the living spectacle of an admitted unbelief destroys the

---

* [Probably George Palmer (1829—1917), British sea captain, whose book *Kidnapping in the South Seas: Being a Narrative of a Three Months' Cruise of* H.M. Ship Rosario (Edinburgh: Edmonston & Douglas, 1871) discusses the Fiji.—*Ed.*]

binding authority of religious custom and snaps the social cord.

Thus we see the use of a sort of "preliminary" age in societies, when trade is bad because it prevents the separation of nations, because it infuses distracting ideas among occupied communities, because it "brings alien minds to alien shores." And as the trade which we now think of as an incalculable good is in that age a formidable evil and destructive calamity; so war and conquest, which we commonly and justly see to be now evils, are in that age often singular benefits and great advantages. It is only by the competition of customs that bad customs can be eliminated and good customs multiplied. Conquest is the premium given by nature to those national characters which their national customs have made most fit to win in war, and in many most material respects those winning characters are really the best characters. The characters which do win in war are the characters which we should wish to win in war.

Similarly, the best institutions have a natural military advantage over bad institutions. The first great victory of civilization was the conquest of nations with ill-defined families having legal descent through the mother only, by nations of definite families tracing descent through the father as well as the mother, or through the father only. Such compact families are a much better basis for military discipline than the ill-bound families which indeed seem hardly to be families at all, where "paternity" is, for tribal purposes, an unrecognized idea, and where only the physical fact of "maternity" is thought to be certain enough to be the foundation of law or custom. The nations with a thoroughly compacted family system have "possessed the earth"; that is, they have taken all the finest districts in the most competed-for parts; and the nations with loose systems have been merely left to mountain ranges and lonely islands. The family system, and that in its highest form, has been so exclusively the system of civilization that literature hardly recognizes any other, and that, if it were not for the living testimony of a great multitude of scattered communities which are "fashioned after the structure of the elder world," we should hardly admit the possibility of something so contrary to all which we have lived amongst and which we have been used to think of. After such an example of the fragmentary nature of the evidence it is in comparison easy to believe that hundreds of strange institutions may have passed away and have left behind them not only no memorial, but not even a trace or a vestige to help the imagination to figure what they were.

I cannot expand the subject, but in the same way the better religions have had a great physical advantage, if I may say so, over the worse. They have given what I may call a *confidence in the universe*. The savage subjected to a mean superstition is afraid to walk simply about the world—he cannot do *this* because it is ominous, or he must do *that* because it is lucky, or he cannot do anything at all till the gods have spoken and given him leave to begin. But under the higher religions there is no similar slavery, and no similar terror. The belief of the Greek:

εἷς οἰωνὸς ἄριστος ἀμύνεσθαι περὶ πάτρης.*

the belief of the Roman that he was to trust in the gods of

* ["The one best omen is to fight for the fatherland," *Iliad* XII:243.—*Ed.*]

191

Rome, for those gods are stronger than all others; the belief of Cromwell's soldiery that they were "to trust in God and keep their powder dry," are great steps in upward progress, using progress in its narrowest sense. They all enabled those who believed them "to take the world as it comes," to be guided by no unreal reason, and to be limited by no mystic scruple; whenever they found anything to do, to do it with their might. And more directly what I may call the *fortifying* religions—that is to say, those which lay the plainest stress on the manly parts of morality—upon valor, on truth and industry have had plainly the most obvious effect in strengthening the races which believed them, and in making those races the winning races.

No doubt many sorts of primitive improvement are pernicious to war; an exquisite sense of beauty, a love of meditation, a tendency to cultivate the force of the mind at the expense of the force of the body, for example, help in their respective degrees to make men less warlike than they would otherwise be. But these are the virtues of other ages. The first work of the first ages is to bind men together in the strong bond of a rough, coarse, harsh custom; and the incessant conflict of nations effects this in the best way. Every nation is a "hereditary cooperative group," bound by a fixed custom; and out of those groups those conquer which have the most binding and most invigorating customs, and these are, as a rough rule, the best customs. The majority of the "groups" which win and conquer are better than the majority of those which fail and perish, and thus the first world grew better and was improved.

This early customary world no doubt continued for ages. The first history delineates great monarchies, each composed of a hundred customary groups, all of which believed themselves to be of enormous antiquity, and all of which must have existed for very many generations. The first historical world is not a new-looking thing but a very ancient, and according to principle it is necessary that it should exist for ages. If human nature was to be gradually improved, each generation must be born better tamed, more calm, more capable of civilization—in a word, more legal than the one before it, and such inherited improvements are always slow and dubious. Though a few gifted people may advance much, the mass of each generation can improve but very little on the generation which preceded it; and even the slight improvement so gained is liable to be destroyed by some mysterious atavism—some strange recurrence to a primitive past. Long ages of dreary monotony are the first facts in the history of human communities, but those ages were not lost to mankind, for it was then that was formed the comparatively gentle and guidable thing which we now call human nature.

And indeed the greatest difficulty is not in preserving such a world but in ending it. We have brought in the yoke of custom to improve the world, and in the world the custom sticks. In a thousand cases—in the great majority of cases—the progress of mankind has been arrested in this its earliest shape; it has been closely embalmed in a mummy-like imitation of its primitive existence. I have endeavored to show in what manner, and how slowly, and in how few cases this yoke of custom was removed. It was "government by discussion" which broke the bond of ages and set free the originality of mankind. Then, and then only, the motives which Lord Macaulay counted on to secure the progress of mankind, in fact, begin to work; *then* "the tendency in every man to ameliorate his condition" begins to be important, because then man can alter his condition while before he is pegged down by ancient usage; *then* the tendency in each mechanical art towards perfection begins to have force, because the artist is at last allowed to seek perfection, after having been forced for ages to move in the straight furrow of the old fixed way.

As soon as this great step upwards is once made, all, or almost all, the higher gifts and graces of humanity have a rapid and a definite effect on "verifiable progress"—on progress in the narrowest, because in the most universally admitted, sense of the term. Success in life, then, depends, as we have seen, more than anything else on "animated moderation," on a certain combination of energy of mind and balance of mind, hard to attain and harder to keep. And this subtle excellence is aided by all the finer graces of humanity. It is a matter of common observation that, though often separated, fine taste and fine judgment go very much together, and especially that a man with gross want of taste, though he may act sensibly and correctly for a while, is yet apt to break out, sooner or later, into gross practical error. In metaphysics, probably both taste and judgment involve what is termed "poise of mind"— that is, the power of true passiveness—the faculty of "waiting" till the stream of impressions, whether those of life or those of art, have done all that they have to do, and cut their full type plainly upon the mind. The ill-judging and the untasteful are both over-eager; both move too quick and blur the image. In this way the union between a subtle sense of beauty and a subtle discretion in conduct is a natural one, because it rests on the common possession of a fine power, though, in matter of fact, that union may be often disturbed. A complex sea of forces and passions troubles men in life and action, which in the calmer region of art are hardly to be felt at all. And, therefore, the cultivation of a fine taste tends to promote the function of a fine judgment, which is a main help in the complex world of civilized existence. Just so too the manner in which the more delicate parts of religion daily work in producing that "moderation" which, upon the whole, and as a rule, is essential to long success, defining success even in its most narrow and mundane way, might be worked out in a hundred cases, though it would not suit these pages. Many of the finer intellectual tastes have a similar restraining effect; they prevent, or tend to prevent, a greedy voracity after the good things of life, which makes both men and nations in excessive haste to be rich and famous, often makes them do too much and do it ill, and so often leaves them at last without money and without respect.

But there is no need to expand this further. The principle is plain that, though these better and higher graces of humanity are impediments and encumbrances in the early fighting period, yet that in the later era they are among the greatest helps and benefits, and that as soon as governments by discussion have become strong enough to secure a stable existence, and as soon as they have broken the fixed rule of old custom, and have awakened the dormant inventiveness of men, then, for the first time, almost every part of human nature begins to spring forward, and begins to contribute its quota even to the narrowest, even to "verifiable" progress. And this is the true reason of all those panegyrics on liberty which are often so measured in expression but are in essence so true to life and nature. Liberty is the strengthening and developing power—the light and heat of political nature; and when some "Caesarism" exhibits as it sometimes will an originality of mind, it is only because it has managed to make its own the products of past free times or neighboring free countries; and even that originality is only brief and frail, and after a little while, when tested by a generation or two, in time of need it falls away.

In a complete investigation of all the conditions of "verifiable progress," much else would have to be set out; for example, science has secrets of her own. Nature does not wear her most useful lessons on her sleeve; she only yields her most productive secrets, those which yield the most wealth and the most "fruit," to those who have gone through a long process of preliminary abstraction. To make a person really understand the "laws of motion" is not easy, and to solve even simple problems in abstract dynamics is to most people exceedingly hard. And yet it is on these out-of-the-way investigations, so to speak, that the art of navigation, all physical astronomy, and all the theory of physical movements at last depend. But no nation would beforehand have thought that in so curious a manner such great secrets were to be discovered. And many nations, therefore, which get on the wrong track may be distanced—supposing there to be no communication by some nation not better than any of them which happens to stumble on the right track. If there were no "Bradshaw"* and no one knew the time at which trains started, a man who caught the express would not be a wiser or a more business-like man than he who missed it, and yet he would arrive whole hours sooner at the capital

* [English railroad time table, first published in 1839 and named for George Bradshaw (1801–1853).—*Ed.*]

both are going to. And unless I misread the matter, such was often the case with early knowledge. At any rate before a complete theory of "verifiable progress" could be made, it would have to be settled whether this is so or not, and the conditions of the development of physical science would have to be fully stated; obviously you cannot explain the development of human comfort unless you know the way in which men learn and discover comfortable things. Then again, for a complete discussion, whether of progress or degradation, a whole course of analysis is necessary as to the effect of natural agencies on man, and of change in those agencies. But upon these I cannot touch; the only way to solve these great problems is to take them separately. I only profess to explain what seem to me the political prerequisites of progress, and especially of early progress. I do this the rather because the subject is insufficiently examined, so that even if my views are found to be faulty, the discussion upon them may bring out others which are truer and better.

Selected Bibliography

PRIMARY SOURCES

The Works of Walter Bagehot. Edited by Forrest Morgan, five volumes (Hartford: The Travelers Insurance Company, 1889). Curiously, this American edition, published at the instigation of the head of the Travelers Insurance Company, was the first collected edition of Bagehot's works to appear. It includes memoirs by Bagehot's lifelong friend Richard Holt Hutton.

The Works and Life of Walter Bagehot. Edited by Mrs. Russell Barrington, ten volumes (London: Longmans, Green and Co., 1915). This edition contains nine volumes of material by Bagehot. The tenth volume is a biography of Bagehot by Mrs. Russell Barrington, Bagehot's sister-in-law.

The Love Letters of Walter Bagehot and Eliza Wilson. Written from November 10, 1857, to April 23, 1858. Edited by Mrs. Russell Barrington (London: Faber and Faber, 1933).

The Collected Works of Walter Bagehot. Edited by Norman St. John-Stevas, fifteen volumes (London: The Economist; and Cambridge, Massachusetts: Harvard University Press, 1965–1986). This monumental and painstaking edition, which features superb introductions by various scholars, is arranged as follows: Literary Essays, Volumes I & II; Historical Essays, Volumes III & IV; Political Essays, Volumes V–VIII; Economic Essays, Volumes IX–XI; Letters, Volumes XI–XIII; Miscellany, Volumes XIV–XV.

Physics and Politics. Edited with an introduction by Jacques Barzun (New York: Alfred A. Knopf, 1948). This edition, now out of print, carries a fine introduction by the historian Jacques Barzun.

The Best of Bagehot. Edited with an introduction by Ruth Dudley Edwards (London: Hamish Hamilton, 1993). An appreciative miscellany, stronger on tidbits than extended passages.

BACKGROUND AND SECONDARY SOURCES

Briggs, Asa. *Victorian People: A Reassessment of Persons and Themes, 1851–67,* revised edition (Chicago: The University fo Chicago Press, 1972). A standard work that includes "Trollope, Bagehot, and the English Constitution," which presents Trollope and Bagehot as "the two writers who most surely described the essentials of [English] life in the late fifties and sixties."

Brinton, Crane. *English Political Thought in the Nineteenth Century* (New York: Harper and Row, 1962). This classic overview, first published in 1933, contains an excellent chapter on Bagehot as an exemplar of English common sense with "a proper feeling for the twsitings and turnigns of human nature in politics."

Buchan, Alastair. *The Spare Chancellor: The Life of Walter Bagehot* (East Lansing, Michigan: Michigan State University Press, 1960). The fullest biography of Bagehot yet to appear.

Gross, John. *The Rise and Fall of the Man of Letters: English Literary Life Since 1800,* new edition (Chicago: Ivan R. Dee, 1992). This superlative study of modern English literary culture, originally published in 1969, provides an excellent account of the intellectual milieu out of which Bagehot arose and to which he contributed.

Himmelfarb, Gertrude. "Walter Bagehot: A Common Man

with Uncommon Ideas," in *Victorian Minds: A Study in Intellectuals in Crisis and Ideologies in Transition* (Chicago: Ivan R. Dee, 1995). First published in 1968, this sensitive and well-informed essay emphasizes Bagehot's "dual vision," his intellectual and characterological subtlety.

St. John-Stevas, Norman. *Walter Bagehot: A Study of His Life and Thought Together with a Selection from His Political Writings* (Bloomington: Indiana University Press, 1959). An excellent biographical introduction and consideration of Bagehot's thought, followed by a generous selection from his writings, by the scholar who has done more than anyone to renew interest in Bagehot.

————. "Walter Bagehot" (London: Published for the British Council and the National Book League by Longmans, Green & Co., 1963). A brief, anecdotal account of Bagehot's career and importance.

Sisson, C. H. *The Case of Walter Bagehot* (London: Faber and Faber, 1972). An intelligent though largely hostile account of Bagehot's thought, emphasizing the elements of calculation and cynicism in Bagehot's character.

Stephen, Sir Leslie. "Walter Bagehot," in *Studies of a Biographer*, Second Series, Vol. III (London: Duckworth & Co., 1902). A thoughtful essay by the distinguished biographer and editor of the *Dictionary of National Biography*.

Sullivan, Harry R. *Walter Bagehot* (Boston: Twayne Publishers, 1975). A brief, reliable introduction to Bagehot's work in the Twayne's English authors series.

Young, G. M. "The Greatest Victorian," in *Today and Yesterday: Collected Essays and Addresses* (London: Rupert Hart-Davis, 1948). A classic and often-referred-to essay on Bagehot by a great scholar of Victorian life.

Index

Index

Index

French Revolution, 28–30, 137,
    147, 149
Fuegians, 92

Galton, Sir Francis, 47, 124
Gamblers, 116–117
Gaul, 44
Geology, 4
Germany, nations of, 161;
    peoples of, 34, 43, 62, 65;
    tribes of, 27, 43, 155
Gibbon, Edward, IX, XII–XIII
Gladstone, William Ewart, XI,
    XVIII, 19, 83, 105, 150
Goethe, Johann Wolfgang von,
    IX, 150
Goths, 97
Government, change of, 99; by
    discussion, XXX V, 141, 143,
    158, 169, 171, 176, 179, 193,
    195; forms of, 62; free, 172,
    179–180; habits of, 89;
    importance of rule for, 25;
    parliamentary, 170
Grant, Ulysses S., 134
Greece, ancient, 142, 148–150,
    189, 191; cities in Asia of,
    159; history of, 37; Homeric,
    19, 45, 62; peoples, 97;
    republics of, 141; states of,
    22; thought in, 25
Grey, Lord, XVIII
Grote, George, 27, 142–143,
    150–151

Habit, XXIX, 96; of discussion,
    146; of mind, 103, 120; see
    also Custom

Hamilton, Sir William, 183
Hampden, John, 178
Harrison, Frederic, 53
Hartley, David, 8
Hebrew patriarchs, 13–15
Herodotus, 76, 99, 151
Himmelfarb, Gertrude, XX–XXI
Hindoos, 14, 66, 140
Holland, 158
Homer, 15, 18–19, 21, 24, 26,
    105, 150, 177, 191
House of Commons, 65
Hutton, Richard Holt, XVI–XVIII
Huxley, Aldous, 7
Huxley, Thomas H., XXVII, 7,
    182

Imitation, in literature, 30–34,
    81–82; in nation-making,
    34–38, 80–96 passim, 130
India, army in, 42; English in,
    126, 129, 139; hill, 49; hill
    tribes of, 40
Individuation, 174
Indo-Europeans, 14
Inheritance, special laws of, 9–10
Inquirer, The (newspaper),
    XXIII–XXV
Instincts, 108–109; family,
    111–112
Institutions, alteration of, 89;
    military advantages of, 190;
    provisional, XXXIV, 67–69
Ireland, 173; peoples of, 34
Isaac, 68

Jacob, 68
Jamaica, 64

Index

Index

Index

211